I0772433

TRIVIA
QUIZ
BOOK

ISBN: 9798389043961
Imprint: Independently published

1- What is the most popular beer style in the world?
A) Lager
B) Ale

2- What is the most widely consumed alcoholic beverage in the world?
A) Beer
B) Wine

3- What is the oldest beer brand in the world?
A) Stella Artois
B) Weihenstephaner

4- What is the proper serving temperature for most beers?
A) 40-45°F
B) 60-65°F

5- What is the most common ingredient in beer?
A) Water
B) Hops

6- What is the main difference between ale and lager?
A) Fermentation temperature
B) Hops content

7- What is the strongest beer in the world?
A) Sam Adams Utopias
B) Brewdog The End of History

8- What is the name for the process of steeping malted grains in hot water to extract sugars for brewing beer?
A) Mashing
B) Fermenting

9- What is the main ingredient that gives beer its bitter flavor?
A) Hops
B) Yeast

10- What is the name for the tool used to open a beer bottle?
A) Bottle opener
B) Cap remover

11- What is the name for the process of carbonating beer?
A) Conditioning
B) Distilling

12- What is the name of the German law that regulates beer production?
A) Reinheitsgebot
B) Weihenstephaner

13- What is the name of the tool used to measure the alcohol content of beer?
A) Hydrometer
B) Refractometer

14- What is the most popular beer brand in the United States?
A) Budweiser
B) Coors Light

15- What is the name for the process of adding extra hops during the brewing process to increase bitterness and aroma?
A) Dry hopping
B) Wet hopping

16- What is the proper glassware for serving a pilsner?
A) Tulip glass
B) Pilsner glass

17- What is the name of the process of filtering out yeast and other particles from beer before bottling or kegging?
A) Clarifying
B) Carbonating

18- What is the name of the organization that certifies beers as organic?
A) USDA
B) Oregon Tilth

19- What is the main ingredient in beer that gives it its color?
A) Malt
B) Hops

20- What is the name of the process of aging beer in barrels previously used for wine or spirits?
A) Barrel aging
B) Bottle conditioning

21- What is the most popular beer brand in Mexico?
A) Corona
B) Modelo

22- What is the name of the process of fermenting beer in the bottle or can in which it is sold?
A) Bottle conditioning
B) Secondary fermentation

23- What is the most popular beer style in the United States?
A) IPA
B) Stout

24- What is the name for the process of heating the wort to a temperature that stops enzyme activity and creates a stable liquid suitable for fermentation?
A) Boiling
B) Mashing

25- What is the most popular beer brand in the world by sales volume?
A) Budweiser
B) Snow

ANSWERS

1- What is the most popular beer style in the world?
A) Lager (Answer)
B) Ale

2- What is the most widely consumed alcoholic beverage in the world?
A) Beer (Answer)
B) Wine

3- What is the oldest beer brand in the world?
A) Stella Artois
B) Weihenstephaner (Answer)

4- What is the proper serving temperature for most beers?
A) 40-45°F (Answer)
B) 60-65°F

5- What is the most common ingredient in beer?
A) Water (Answer)
B) Hops

6- What is the main difference between ale and lager?
A) Fermentation temperature (Answer)
B) Hops content

7- What is the strongest beer in the world?
A) Sam Adams Utopias
B) Brewdog The End of History (Answer)

8- What is the name for the process of steeping malted grains in hot water to extract sugars for brewing beer?
A) Mashing (Answer)
B) Fermenting

9- What is the main ingredient that gives beer its bitter flavor?
A) Hops (Answer)
B) Yeast

10- What is the name for the tool used to open a beer bottle?
A) Bottle opener (Answer)
B) Cap remover

11- What is the name for the process of carbonating beer?
A) Conditioning (Answer)
B) Distilling

12- What is the name of the German law that regulates beer production?
A) Reinheitsgebot (Answer)
B) Weihenstephaner

13- What is the name of the tool used to measure the alcohol content of beer?
A) Hydrometer (Answer)
B) Refractometer

14- What is the most popular beer brand in the United States?
A) Budweiser
B) Coors Light (Answer)

15- What is the name for the process of adding extra hops during the brewing process to increase bitterness and aroma?
A) Dry hopping (Answer)
B) Wet hopping

16- What is the proper glassware for serving a pilsner?
A) Tulip glass
B) Pilsner glass (Answer)

17- What is the name of the process of filtering out yeast and other particles from beer before bottling or kegging?
A) Clarifying (Answer)
B) Carbonating

18- What is the name of the organization that certifies beers as organic?
A) USDA
B) Oregon Tilth (Answer)

19- What is the main ingredient in beer that gives it its color?
A) Malt (Answer)
B) Hops

20- What is the name of the process of aging beer in barrels previously used for wine or spirits?
A) Barrel aging (Answer)
B) Bottle conditioning

21- What is the most popular beer brand in Mexico?
A) Corona (Answer)
B) Modelo

22- What is the name of the process of fermenting beer in the bottle or can in which it is sold?
A) Bottle conditioning (Answer)
B) Secondary fermentation

23- What is the most popular beer style in the United States?
A) IPA (Answer)
B) Stout

24- What is the name for the process of heating the wort to a temperature that stops enzyme activity and creates a stable liquid suitable for fermentation?
A) Boiling (Answer)
B) Mashing

25- What is the most popular beer brand in the world by sales volume?
A) Budweiser
B) Snow (Answer)

1- What is the name of the dog breed that is often associated with fire departments and rescue work?
A) Dalmatian
B) Poodle

2- What is the name of the dog breed that is often used as a guide dog for the blind?
A) Labrador Retriever
B) Chihuahua

3- What is the name of the dog breed that is often used for hunting?
A) Beagle
B) Pomeranian

4- What is the name of the dog breed that is often used for herding livestock?
A) Border Collie
B) Shih Tzu

5- What is the name of the breed that is often used as a guard dog?
A) German Shepherd
B) Yorkshire Terrier

6- What is the name of the breed that is known for its wrinkly skin and short legs?
A) Bulldog
B) Greyhound

7- What is the name of the breed that is known for its fluffy coat and curly tail?
A) Pomeranian
B) Boxer

8- What is the name of the breed that is known for its long, silky hair?
A) Afghan Hound
B) Bichon Frise

9- What is the name of the breed that is known for its smushed face and snoring?
A) Pug
B) Siberian Husky

10- What is the name of the breed that is known for its small size and big ears?
A) Chihuahua
B) Doberman Pinscher

11- What is the name of the breed that is known for its curly hair and love of water?
A) Poodle
B) Boxer

12- What is the name of the breed that is known for its loyalty and devotion to its owner?
A) Akita
B) Maltese

13- What is the name of the breed that is known for its pointed ears and wolf-like appearance?
A) Siberian Husky
B) Golden Retriever

14- What is the name of the breed that is known for its affectionate nature and wrinkled forehead?
A) Boxer
B) Dachshund

15- What is the name of the breed that is known for its short legs and long body?
A) Dachshund
B) Shih Tzu

16- What is the name of the breed that is known for its curly fur and small size?
A) Bichon Frise
B) Great Dane

17- What is the name of the breed that is known for its spotted coat and high energy?
A) Australian Cattle Dog
B) Boston Terrier

18- What is the name of the breed that is known for its friendly nature and wagging tail?
A) Golden Retriever
B) Rottweiler

19- What is the name of the breed that is known for its muscular build and protective nature?
A) Doberman Pinscher
B) Cavalier King Charles Spaniel

20- What is the name of the breed that is known for its shaggy coat and ability to swim?
A) Portuguese Water Dog
B) Shetland Sheepdog

ANSWERS

1- What is the name of the breed that is often associated with fire departments and rescue work?
A) Dalmatian (Answer)
B) Poodle

2- What is the name of the breed that is often used as a guide dog for the blind?
A) Labrador Retriever (Answer)
B) Chihuahua

3- What is the name of the breed that is often used for hunting?
A) Beagle (Answer)
B) Pomeranian

4- What is the name of the breed that is often used for herding livestock?
A) Border Collie (Answer)
B) Shih Tzu

5- What is the name of the breed that is often used as a guard dog?
A) German Shepherd (Answer)
B) Yorkshire Terrier

6- What is the name of the breed that is known for its wrinkly skin and short legs?
A) Bulldog (Answer)
B) Greyhound

7- What is the name of the breed that is known for its fluffy coat and curly tail?
A) Pomeranian (Answer)
B) Boxer

8- What is the name of the breed that is known for its long, silky hair?
A) Afghan Hound (Answer)
B) Bichon Frise

9- What is the name of the breed that is known for its smushed face and snoring?
A) Pug (Answer)
B) Siberian Husky

10- What is the name of the breed that is known for its small size and big ears?
A) Chihuahua (Answer)
B) Doberman Pinscher

11- What is the name of the breed that is known for its curly hair and love of water?
A) Poodle (Answer)
B) Boxer

12- What is the name of the breed that is known for its loyalty and devotion to its owner?
A) Akita (Answer)
B) Maltese

13- What is the name of the breed that is known for its pointed ears and wolf-like appearance?
A) Siberian Husky (Answer)
B) Golden Retriever

14- What is the name of the breed that is known for its affectionate nature and wrinkled forehead?
A) Boxer (Answer)
B) Dachshund

15- What is the name of the breed that is known for its short legs and long body?
A) Dachshund (Answer)
B) Shih Tzu

16- What is the name of the breed that is known for its curly fur and small size?
A) Bichon Frise (Answer)
B) Great Dane

17- What is the name of the breed that is known for its spotted coat and high energy?
A) Australian Cattle Dog (Answer)
B) Boston Terrier

18- What is the name of the breed that is known for its friendly nature and wagging tail?
A) Golden Retriever (Answer)
B) Rottweiler

19- What is the name of the breed that is known for its muscular build and protective nature?
A) Doberman Pinscher (Answer)
B) Cavalier King Charles Spaniel

20- What is the name of the breed that is known for its shaggy coat and ability to swim?
A) Portuguese Water Dog (Answer)
B) Shetland Sheepdog

1- What is the largest land animal in Africa?
A) Giraffe
B) Elephant

2- What is the smallest antelope in Africa?
A) Dik-dik
B) Springbok

3- What is the fastest land animal in Africa?
A) Cheetah
B) Lion

4- What is the largest carnivore in Africa?
A) Lion
B) Spotted hyena

5- What is the largest primate in Africa?
A) Chimpanzee
B) Gorilla

6- What is the tallest animal in Africa?
A) Ostrich
B) Giraffe

7- What is the largest rodent in Africa?
A) Naked mole-rat
B) African giant pouched rat

8- What is the most venomous snake in Africa?
A) Black mamba
B) Gaboon viper

9- What is the largest bird in Africa?
A) Ostrich
B) Vulture

10- What is the most dangerous animal in Africa?
A) Lion
B) Mosquito

11- What is the largest fish in Africa's freshwater rivers?
A) Tigerfish
B) Nile perch

12- What is the smallest carnivore in Africa?
A) Meerkat
B) Dwarf mongoose

13- What is the only species of bear found in Africa?
A) Black bear
B) Sun bear

14- What is the largest land-dwelling crab in Africa?
A) Coconut crab
B) Giant land crab

15- What is the largest reptile in Africa?
A) Nile crocodile
B) African rock python

16- What is the smallest mammal in Africa?
A) Bat-eared fox
B) Pygmy shrew

17- What is the largest land animal predator in Africa?
A) Lion
B) Spotted hyena

18- What is the largest species of antelope in Africa?
A) Eland
B) Kudu

19- What is the largest species of baboon in Africa?
A) Yellow baboon
B) Chacma baboon

20- What is the smallest species of zebra in Africa?
A) Plains zebra
B) Mountain zebra

21- What is the largest species of otter in Africa?
A) Giant otter
B) Cape clawless otter

22- What is the most endangered species of rhino in Africa?
A) Black rhino
B) White rhino

23- What is the largest species of turtle in Africa?
A) Leatherback turtle
B) Nile softshell turtle

24- What is the largest species of mongoose in Africa?
A) Banded mongoose
B) White-tailed mongoose

25- What is the most endangered species of giraffe in Africa?
A) Rothschild's giraffe
B) Masai giraffe

ANSWERS

1- What is the largest land animal in Africa?
A) Giraffe
B) Elephant (Answer)

2- What is the smallest antelope in Africa?
A) Dik-dik (Answer)
B) Springbok

3- What is the fastest land animal in Africa?
A) Cheetah (Answer)
B) Lion

4- What is the largest carnivore in Africa?
A) Lion
B) Spotted hyena (Answer)

5- What is the largest primate in Africa?
A) Chimpanzee
B) Gorilla (Answer)

6- What is the tallest animal in Africa?
A) Ostrich
B) Giraffe (Answer)

7- What is the largest rodent in Africa?
A) Naked mole-rat
B) African giant pouched rat (Answer)

8- What is the most venomous snake in Africa?
A) Black mamba (Answer)
B) Gaboon viper

9- What is the largest bird in Africa?
A) Ostrich (Answer)
B) Vulture

10- What is the most dangerous animal in Africa?
A) Lion
B) Mosquito (Answer)

11- What is the largest fish in Africa's freshwater rivers?
A) Tigerfish (Answer)
B) Nile perch

12- What is the smallest carnivore in Africa?
A) Meerkat
B) Dwarf mongoose (Answer)

13- What is the only species of bear found in Africa?
A) Black bear
B) Sun bear (Answer)

14- What is the largest land-dwelling crab in Africa?
A) Coconut crab
B) Giant land crab (Answer)

15- What is the largest reptile in Africa?
A) Nile crocodile (Answer)
B) African rock python

16- What is the smallest mammal in Africa?
A) Bat-eared fox
B) Pygmy shrew (Answer)

17- What is the largest land animal predator in Africa?
A) Lion
B) Spotted hyena (Answer)

18- What is the largest species of antelope in Africa?
A) Eland (Answer)
B) Kudu

19- What is the largest species of baboon in Africa?
A) Yellow baboon
B) Chacma baboon (Answer)

20- What is the smallest species of zebra in Africa?
A) Plains zebra
B) Mountain zebra (Answer)

21- What is the largest species of otter in Africa?
A) Giant otter
B) Cape clawless otter (Answer)

22- What is the most endangered species of rhino in Africa?
A) Black rhino (Answer)
B) White rhino

23- What is the largest species of turtle in Africa?
A) Leatherback turtle
B) Nile softshell turtle (Answer)

24- What is the largest species of mongoose in Africa?
A) Banded mongoose
B) White-tailed mongoose (Answer)

25- What is the most endangered species of giraffe in Africa?
A) Rothschild's giraffe (Answer)
B) Masai giraffe

1- Who played the lead role in the movie "Forrest Gump"?
A) Tom Hanks
B) Brad Pitt

2- Who played the character of Harry Potter in the Harry Potter film series?
A) Daniel Radcliffe
B) Robert Pattinson

3- Who played the character of Iron Man in the Marvel Cinematic Universe?
A) Robert Downey Jr.
B) Chris Evans

4- Who played the character of The Joker in "The Dark Knight"?
A) Heath Ledger
B) Joaquin Phoenix

5- Who played the character of James Bond in the 007 series of movies?
A) Sean Connery
B) Pierce Brosnan

6- Who played the character of Katniss Everdeen in "The Hunger Games" series?
A) Jennifer Lawrence
B) Emma Stone

7- Who played the character of Jack Dawson in "Titanic"?
A) Leonardo DiCaprio
B) Johnny Depp

8- Who played the character of Neo in "The Matrix"?
A) Keanu Reeves
B) Brad Pitt

9- Who played the character of Willy Wonka in the movie "Charlie and the Chocolate Factory"?
A) Johnny Depp
B) Tom Hanks

10- Who played the character of Ellen Ripley in the "Alien" film series?
A) Sigourney Weaver
B) Sandra Bullock

11- Who played the character of Wolverine in the "X-Men" film series?
A) Hugh Jackman
B) Chris Hemsworth

12- Who played the character of Hermione Granger in the Harry Potter film series?
A) Emma Watson
B) Kristen Stewart

13- Who played the character of Luke Skywalker in the original "Star Wars" trilogy?
A) Mark Hamill
B) Harrison Ford

14- Who played the character of Captain Jack Sparrow in the "Pirates of the Caribbean" series?
A) Johnny Depp
B) Tom Cruise

15- Who played the character of John McClane in the "Die Hard" film series?
A) Bruce Willis
B) Sylvester Stallone

16- Who played the character of Tony Montana in the movie "Scarface"?
A) Al Pacino
B) Robert De Niro

17- Who played the character of Vito Corleone in "The Godfather"?
A) Marlon Brando
B) Robert Redford

18- Who played the character of Andy Dufresne in "The Shawshank Redemption"?
A) Tim Robbins
B) Morgan Freeman

19- Who played the character of Clarice Starling in "The Silence of the Lambs"?
A) Jodie Foster
B) Sandra Bullock

20- Who played the character of Rocky Balboa in the "Rocky" film series?
A) Sylvester Stallone
B) Arnold Schwarzenegger

21- Who played the character of Hannibal Lecter in "The Silence of the Lambs"?
A) Anthony Hopkins
B) Jack Nicholson

22- Who played the character of The Bride in "Kill Bill"?
A) Uma Thurman
B) Charlize Theron

ANSWERS

1- Who played the lead role in the movie "Forrest Gump"?
A) Tom Hanks (Answer)
B) Brad Pitt

2- Who played the character of Harry Potter in the Harry Potter film series?
A) Daniel Radcliffe (Answer)
B) Robert Pattinson

3- Who played the character of Iron Man in the Marvel Cinematic Universe?
A) Robert Downey Jr. (Answer)
B) Chris Evans

4- Who played the character of The Joker in "The Dark Knight"?
A) Heath Ledger (Answer)
B) Joaquin Phoenix

5- Who played the character of James Bond in the 007 series of movies?
A) Sean Connery (Answer)
B) Pierce Brosnan

6- Who played the character of Katniss Everdeen in "The Hunger Games" series?
A) Jennifer Lawrence (Answer)
B) Emma Stone

7- Who played the character of Jack Dawson in "Titanic"?
A) Leonardo DiCaprio (Answer)
B) Johnny Depp

8- Who played the character of Neo in "The Matrix"?
A) Keanu Reeves (Answer)
B) Brad Pitt

9- Who played the character of Willy Wonka in the movie "Charlie and the Chocolate Factory"?
A) Johnny Depp (Answer)
B) Tom Hanks

10- Who played the character of Ellen Ripley in the "Alien" film series?
A) Sigourney Weaver (Answer)
B) Sandra Bullock

11- Who played the character of Wolverine in the "X-Men" film series?
A) Hugh Jackman (Answer)
B) Chris Hemsworth

12- Who played the character of Hermione Granger in the Harry Potter film series?
A) Emma Watson (Answer)
B) Kristen Stewart

13- Who played the character of Luke Skywalker in the original "Star Wars" trilogy?
A) Mark Hamill (Answer)
B) Harrison Ford

14- Who played the character of Captain Jack Sparrow in the "Pirates of the Caribbean" series?
A) Johnny Depp (Answer)
B) Tom Cruise

15- Who played the character of John McClane in the "Die Hard" film series?
A) Bruce Willis (Answer)
B) Sylvester Stallone

16- Who played the character of Tony Montana in the movie "Scarface"?
A) Al Pacino (Answer)
B) Robert De Niro

17- Who played the character of Vito Corleone in "The Godfather"?
A) Marlon Brando (Answer)
B) Robert Redford

18- Who played the character of Andy Dufresne in "The Shawshank Redemption"?
A) Tim Robbins (Answer)
B) Morgan Freeman

19- Who played Clarice Starling in "The Silence of the Lambs"?
A) Jodie Foster (Answer)
B) Sandra Bullock

20- Who played the character of Rocky Balboa in the "Rocky" film series?
A) Sylvester Stallone (Answer)
B) Arnold Schwarzenegger

21- Who played Hannibal Lecter in "The Silence of the Lambs"?
A) Anthony Hopkins (Answer)
B) Jack Nicholson

22- Who played the character of The Bride in "Kill Bill"?
A) Uma Thurman (Answer)
B) Charlize Theron

1- What is the chemical symbol for gold?
A) Ag
B) Au

2- Which precious metal is known for its use in electrical wiring and is a good conductor of electricity?
A) Gold
B) Silver

3- What is the name of the alloy made from copper and zinc, which is often used in making jewelry?
A) Stainless steel
B) Brass

4- Which precious metal is the most abundant in the Earth's crust?
A) Platinum
B) Silver

5- What is the chemical symbol for platinum?
A) Pt
B) Pb

6- Which precious metal is often used in dentistry because of its durability and resistance to corrosion?
A) Silver
B) Palladium

7- What is the name of the process used to extract gold from ore?
A) Smelting
B) Filtration

8- Which precious metal is often used in jewelry and is known for its deep red color?
A) Gold
B) Rose gold

9- What is the name of the alloy made from gold and copper, which is often used in making jewelry?
A) Bronze
B) Rose gold

10- Which precious metal is often used in catalytic converters in automobiles to reduce emissions?
A) Platinum
B) Palladium

11- What is the chemical symbol for silver?
A) Ag
B) Au

12- Which precious metal is often used in the aerospace industry due to its resistance to high temperatures?
A) Platinum
B) Titanium

13- What is the name of the process used to extract silver from ore?
A) Electroplating
B) Cyanide leaching

14- Which precious metal is often used in mirrors because of its high reflectivity?
A) Platinum
B) Silver

15- What is the name of the process used to extract palladium from ore?
A) Carbon adsorption
B) Solvent extraction

16- Which precious metal is often used in making coins and is known for its durability and resistance to corrosion?
A) Gold
B) Platinum

17- What is the name of the alloy made from gold and silver, which is often used in making jewelry?
A) White gold
B) Sterling silver

18- Which precious metal is often used in electronics due to its ability to resist corrosion and oxidation?
A) Platinum
B) Ruthenium

19- What is the chemical symbol for palladium?
A) Pd
B) Pr

20- Which precious metal is often used in watchmaking due to its durability and resistance to scratches?
A) Platinum
B) Titanium

21- What is the name of the process used to extract copper from ore?
A) Carbon adsorption
B) Froth flotation

22- Which precious metal is often used in making dental implants due to its biocompatibility?
A) Gold
B) Titanium

23- What is the name of the alloy made from gold, copper, and silver, which is often used in making jewelry?
A) Electrum
B) Brass

24- Which precious metal is often used in catalytic converters in diesel engines to reduce emissions?
A) Platinum
B) Rhodium

ANSWERS

1- What is the chemical symbol for gold?
A) Ag
B) Au (Answer)

2- Which precious metal is known for its use in electrical wiring and is a good conductor of electricity?
A) Gold
B) Silver (Answer)

3- What is the name of the alloy made from copper and zinc, which is often used in making jewelry?
A) Stainless steel
B) Brass (Answer)

4- Which precious metal is the most abundant in the Earth's crust?
A) Platinum
B) Silver (Answer)

5- What is the chemical symbol for platinum?
A) Pt (Answer)
B) Pb

6- Which precious metal is often used in dentistry because of its durability and resistance to corrosion?
A) Silver
B) Palladium (Answer)

7- What is the name of the process used to extract gold from ore?
A) Smelting (Answer)
B) Filtration

8- Which precious metal is often used in jewelry and is known for its deep red color?
A) Gold
B) Rose gold (Answer)

9- What is the name of the alloy made from gold and copper, which is often used in making jewelry?
A) Bronze
B) Rose gold (Answer)

10- Which precious metal is often used in catalytic converters in automobiles to reduce emissions?
A) Platinum (Answer)
B) Palladium

11- What is the chemical symbol for silver?
A) Ag (Answer)
B) Au

12- Which precious metal is often used in the aerospace industry due to its resistance to high temperatures?
A) Platinum
B) Titanium (Answer)

13- What is the name of the process used to extract silver from ore?
A) Electroplating
B) Cyanide leaching (Answer)

14- Which precious metal is often used in mirrors because of its high reflectivity?
A) Platinum
B) Silver (Answer)

15- What is the name of the process used to extract palladium from ore?
A) Carbon adsorption
B) Solvent extraction (Answer)

16- Which precious metal is often used in making coins and is known for its durability and resistance to corrosion?
A) Gold
B) Platinum (Answer)

17- What is the name of the alloy made from gold and silver, which is often used in making jewelry?
A) White gold (Answer)
B) Sterling silver

18- Which precious metal is often used in electronics due to its ability to resist corrosion and oxidation?
A) Platinum
B) Ruthenium (Answer)

19- What is the chemical symbol for palladium?
A) Pd (Answer)
B) Pr

20- Which precious metal is often used in watchmaking due to its durability and resistance to scratches?
A) Platinum
B) Titanium (Answer)

21- What is the name of the process used to extract copper from ore?
A) Carbon adsorption
B) Froth flotation (Answer)

22- Which precious metal is often used in making dental implants due to its biocompatibility?
A) Gold
B) Titanium (Answer)

23- What is the name of the alloy made from gold, copper, and silver, which is often used in making jewelry?
A) Electrum (Answer)
B) Brass

24- Which precious metal is often used in catalytic converters in diesel engines to reduce emissions?
A) Platinum (Answer)
B) Rhodium

1- What is the name of the famous physicist who developed the theory of relativity?
A) Albert Einstein
B) Isaac Newton

2- What is the name of the famous artist who painted the Mona Lisa?
A) Leonardo da Vinci
B) Vincent van Gogh

3- What is the name of the famous mathematician who developed the law of gravity?
A) Isaac Newton
B) Galileo Galilei

4- What is the name of the famous scientist who developed the theory of evolution?
A) Charles Darwin
B) Louis Pasteur

5- What is the name of the famous writer who wrote the plays Romeo and Juliet and Hamlet?
A) William Shakespeare
B) Mark Twain

6- What is the name of the famous philosopher who wrote the book The Republic?
A) Plato
B) Aristotle

7- What is the name of the famous artist who painted The Starry Night?
A) Vincent van Gogh
B) Pablo Picasso

8- What is the name of the famous composer who wrote the Ninth Symphony?
A) Ludwig van Beethoven
B) Wolfgang Amadeus Mozart

9- What is the name of the famous inventor who invented the telephone?
A) Alexander Graham Bell
B) Thomas Edison

10- What is the name of the famous author who wrote the book 1984?
A) George Orwell
B) Aldous Huxley

11- What is the name of the famous philosopher who wrote Meditations?
A) Marcus Aurelius
B) René Descartes

12- What is the name of the famous scientist who discovered the laws of motion?
A) Isaac Newton
B) Albert Einstein

13- What is the name of the famous inventor who invented the light bulb?
A) Thomas Edison
B) Alexander Graham Bell

14- What is the name of the famous physicist who developed the first law of thermodynamics?
A) Rudolf Clausius
B) Max Planck

15- What is the name of the famous psychologist who developed the theory of cognitive development?
A) Jean Piaget
B) Sigmund Freud

16- What is the name of the famous astronomer who proposed the heliocentric model of the solar system?
A) Nicolaus Copernicus
B) Galileo Galilei

17- What is the name of the famous novelist who wrote the book Crime and Punishment?
A) Fyodor Dostoevsky
B) Leo Tolstoy

18- What is the name of the famous physicist who discovered the principles of electromagnetism?
A) James Clerk Maxwell
B) Michael Faraday

19- What is the name of the famous scientist who discovered the structure of DNA?
A) James Watson
B) Francis Crick

20- What is the name of the famous philosopher who wrote Thus Spoke Zarathustra?
A) Friedrich Nietzsche
B) Immanuel Kant

ANSWERS

1- What is the name of the famous physicist who developed the theory of relativity?
A) Albert Einstein (Answer)
B) Isaac Newton

2- What is the name of the famous artist who painted the Mona Lisa?
A) Leonardo da Vinci (Answer)
B) Vincent van Gogh

3- What is the name of the famous mathematician who developed the law of gravity?
A) Isaac Newton (Answer)
B) Galileo Galilei

4- What is the name of the famous scientist who developed the theory of evolution?
A) Charles Darwin (Answer)
B) Louis Pasteur

5- What is the name of the famous writer who wrote the plays Romeo and Juliet and Hamlet?
A) William Shakespeare (Answer)
B) Mark Twain

6- What is the name of the famous philosopher who wrote the book The Republic?
A) Plato (Answer)
B) Aristotle

7- What is the name of the famous artist who painted The Starry Night?
A) Vincent van Gogh (Answer)
B) Pablo Picasso

8- What is the name of the famous composer who wrote the Ninth Symphony?
A) Ludwig van Beethoven (Answer)
B) Wolfgang Amadeus Mozart

9- What is the name of the famous inventor who invented the telephone?
A) Alexander Graham Bell (Answer)
B) Thomas Edison

10- What is the name of the famous author who wrote the book 1984?
A) George Orwell (Answer)
B) Aldous Huxley

11- What is the name of the famous philosopher who wrote Meditations?
A) Marcus Aurelius (Answer)
B) René Descartes

12- What is the name of the famous scientist who discovered the laws of motion?
A) Isaac Newton (Answer)
B) Albert Einstein

13- What is the name of the famous inventor who invented the light bulb?
A) Thomas Edison (Answer)
B) Alexander Graham Bell

14- What is the name of the famous physicist who developed the first law of thermodynamics?
A) Rudolf Clausius (Answer)
B) Max Planck

15- What is the name of the famous psychologist who developed the theory of cognitive development?
A) Jean Piaget (Answer)
B) Sigmund Freud

16- What is the name of the famous astronomer who proposed the heliocentric model of the solar system?
A) Nicolaus Copernicus (Answer)
B) Galileo Galilei

17- What is the name of the famous novelist who wrote the book Crime and Punishment?
A) Fyodor Dostoevsky (Answer)
B) Leo Tolstoy

18- What is the name of the famous physicist who discovered the principles of electromagnetism?
A) James Clerk Maxwell (Answer)
B) Michael Faraday

19- What is the name of the famous scientist who discovered the structure of DNA?
A) James Watson (Answer)
B) Francis Crick

20- What is the name of the famous philosopher who wrote Thus Spoke Zarathustra?
A) Friedrich Nietzsche (Answer)
B) Immanuel Kant

1- What is the name of the popular chocolate bar that has a nougat center?
A) Milky Way
B) Snickers

2- What is the name of the popular fruit-flavored candy that comes in a small box with a sliding lid?
A) Nerds
B) Skittles

3- What is the name of the popular hard candy that comes in a wrapper with a yellow and red design?
A) Lifesavers
B) Jolly Ranchers

4- What is the name of the popular chocolate and caramel candy that is chewy and stretchy?
A) Tootsie Roll
B) Milk Duds

5- What is the name of the popular candy that comes in a tube and is shaped like small pellets?
A) Smarties
B) M&M's

6- What is the name of the popular candy that is shaped like small bears and comes in different flavors?
A) Gummy Bears
B) Sour Patch Kids

7- What is the name of the popular candy that comes in a colorful tube and is twisted like a rope?
A) Twizzlers
B) Red Vines

8- What is the name of the popular candy that comes in a wrapper with a red and white stripe design?
A) Peppermint
B) Spearmint

9- What is the name of the popular chocolate bar that is filled with caramel and peanuts?
A) Snickers
B) Milky Way

10- What is the name of the popular chocolate bar that is filled with wafer and covered in chocolate?
A) Kit Kat
B) Twix

11- What is the name of the popular candy that is made with peanut butter and chocolate?
A) Reese's Peanut Butter Cups
B) Butterfinger

12- What is the name of the popular candy that is a mix of chocolate, caramel, and nougat?
A) Milky Way
B) 3 Musketeers

13- What is the name of the popular candy that is a mix of chocolate and peanuts?
A) Snickers
B) Baby Ruth

14- What is the name of the popular candy that comes in a small yellow and orange wrapper and has a peanut butter filling?
A) Butterfinger
B) 100 Grand

15- What is the name of the popular candy that comes in a small blue wrapper and has a tart and sweet flavor?
A) Sour Patch Kids
B) Airheads

16- What is the name of the popular candy that is a mix of chocolate and caramel?
A) Twix
B) 100 Grand

17- What is the name of the popular candy that comes in a small box and has small, chewy, fruit-flavored pieces?
A) Skittles
B) Starburst

18- What is the name of the popular candy that is a mix of chocolate and peanut butter with a crispy center?
A) Reese's Pieces
B) Crunch

19- What is the name of the popular candy that is a mix of chocolate and marshmallow with a graham cracker center?
A) Hershey's S'mores
B) Milky Way

20- What is the name of the popular candy that is a mix of chocolate and nuts?
A) Almond Joy
B) Heath Bar

ANSWERS

1- What is the name of the popular chocolate bar that has a nougat center?
A) Milky Way (Answer)
B) Snickers

2- What is the name of the popular fruit-flavored candy that comes in a small box with a sliding lid?
A) Nerds (Answer)
B) Skittles

3- What is the name of the popular hard candy that comes in a wrapper with a yellow and red design?
A) Lifesavers (Answer)
B) Jolly Ranchers

4- What is the name of the popular chocolate and caramel candy that is chewy and stretchy?
A) Tootsie Roll (Answer)
B) Milk Duds

5- What is the name of the popular candy that comes in a tube and is shaped like small pellets?
A) Smarties (Answer)
B) M&M's

6- What is the name of the popular candy that is shaped like small bears and comes in different flavors?
A) Gummy Bears (Answer)
B) Sour Patch Kids

7- What is the name of the popular candy that comes in a colorful tube and is twisted like a rope?
A) Twizzlers (Answer)
B) Red Vines

8- What is the name of the popular candy that comes in a wrapper with a red and white stripe design?
A) Peppermint (Answer)
B) Spearmint

9- What is the name of the popular chocolate bar that is filled with caramel and peanuts?
A) Snickers (Answer)
B) Milky Way

10- What is the name of the popular chocolate bar that is filled with wafer and covered in chocolate?
A) Kit Kat (Answer)
B) Twix

11- What is the name of the popular candy that is made with peanut butter and chocolate?
A) Reese's Peanut Butter Cups (Answer)
B) Butterfinger

12- What is the name of the popular candy that is a mix of chocolate, caramel, and nougat?
A) Milky Way (Answer)
B) 3 Musketeers

13- What is the name of the popular candy that is a mix of chocolate and peanuts?
A) Snickers (Answer)
B) Baby Ruth

14- What is the name of the popular candy that comes in a small yellow and orange wrapper and has a peanut butter filling?
A) Butterfinger (Answer)
B) 100 Grand

15- What is the name of the popular candy that comes in a small blue wrapper and has a tart and sweet flavor?
A) Sour Patch Kids (Answer)
B) Airheads

16- What is the name of the popular candy that is a mix of chocolate and caramel?
A) Twix (Answer)
B) 100 Grand

17- What is the name of the popular candy that comes in a small box and has small, chewy, fruit-flavored pieces?
A) Skittles (Answer)
B) Starburst

18- What is the name of the popular candy that is a mix of chocolate and peanut butter with a crispy center?
A) Reese's Pieces (Answer)
B) Crunch

19- What is the name of the popular candy that is a mix of chocolate and marshmallow with a graham cracker center?
A) Hershey's S'mores (Answer)
B) Milky Way

20- What is the name of the popular candy that is a mix of chocolate and nuts?
A) Almond Joy (Answer)
B) Heath Bar

1- What is the name of the process used to turn grape juice into wine?
A) Fermentation
B) Distillation

2- What is the name of the type of wine that is made from white grapes?
A) Red wine
B) White wine

3- What is the name of the process used to age wine in oak barrels?
A) Barrel fermentation
B) Barrel aging

4- What is the name of the tool used to remove the cork from a wine bottle?
A) Wine opener
B) Beer opener

5- What is the name of the country that produces the most wine in the world?
A) France
B) Italy

6- What is the name of the type of wine that is made from red grapes?
A) White wine
B) Red wine

7- What is the name of the process used to remove sediment from a bottle of wine?
A) Decanting
B) Filtering

8- What is the name of the tool used to aerate wine by pouring it through a funnel-shaped device?
A) Wine decanter
B) Wine cooler

9- What is the name of the process used to add sugar to wine?
A) Fortification
B) Chaptalization

10- What is the name of the region in France known for producing champagne?
A) Bordeaux
B) Champagne

11- What is the name of the grape used to make Chardonnay wine?
A) Pinot Noir
B) Chardonnay

12- What is the name of the tool used to measure the alcohol content of wine?
A) Alcoholometer
B) Thermometer

13- What is the name of the type of wine that is made from partially dried grapes?
A) Ice wine
B) Amarone

14- What is the name of the tool used to stopper an open bottle of wine?
A) Wine stopper
B) Corkscrew

15- What is the name of the process used to make sweet wines by stopping the fermentation process early?
A) Fortification
B) Arrested fermentation

16- What is the name of the region in California known for producing Cabernet Sauvignon wine?
A) Napa Valley
B) Sonoma County

17- What is the name of the grape used to make Merlot wine?
A) Merlot
B) Cabernet Sauvignon

18- What is the name of the tool used to remove excess air from an open bottle of wine?
A) Wine saver
B) Wine opener

19- What is the name of the type of wine that is made from frozen grapes?
A) Ice wine
B) Port

20- What is the name of the region in Italy known for producing Chianti wine?
A) Tuscany
B) Piedmont

21- What is the name of the process used to add flavor to wine by soaking wood chips in it?
A) Barrel aging
B) Oak infusion

22- What is the name of the tool used to chill a bottle of wine quickly?
A) Wine cooler
B) Ice bucket

23- What is the name of the grape used to make Pinot Noir wine?
A) Cabernet Sauvignon
B) Pinot Noir

24- What is the name of the process used to make sparkling wine by inducing a secondary fermentation in the bottle?
A) Methode champenoise
B) Carbonation

ANSWERS

1- What is the name of the process used to turn grape juice into wine?
A) Fermentation (Answer)
B) Distillation

2- What is the name of the type of wine that is made from white grapes?
A) Red wine
B) White wine (Answer)

3- What is the name of the process used to age wine in oak barrels?
A) Barrel fermentation
B) Barrel aging (Answer)

4- What is the name of the tool used to remove the cork from a wine bottle?
A) Wine opener (Answer)
B) Beer opener

5- What is the name of the country that produces the most wine in the world?
A) France
B) Italy (Answer)

6- What is the name of the type of wine that is made from red grapes?
A) White wine
B) Red wine (Answer)

7- What is the name of the process used to remove sediment from a bottle of wine?
A) Decanting (Answer)
B) Filtering

8- What is the name of the tool used to aerate wine by pouring it through a funnel-shaped device?
A) Wine decanter (Answer)
B) Wine cooler

9- What is the name of the process used to add sugar to wine?
A) Fortification
B) Chaptalization (Answer)

10- What is the name of the region in France known for producing champagne?
A) Bordeaux
B) Champagne (Answer)

11- What is the name of the grape used to make Chardonnay wine?
A) Pinot Noir
B) Chardonnay (Answer)

12- What is the name of the tool used to measure the alcohol content of wine?
A) Alcoholometer (Answer)
B) Thermometer

13- What is the name of the type of wine that is made from partially dried grapes?
A) Ice wine
B) Amarone (Answer)

14- What is the name of the tool used to stopper an open bottle of wine?
A) Wine stopper (Answer)
B) Corkscrew

15- What is the name of the process used to make sweet wines by stopping the fermentation process early?
A) Fortification
B) Arrested fermentation (Answer)

16- What is the name of the region in California known for producing Cabernet Sauvignon wine?
A) Napa Valley (Answer)
B) Sonoma County

17- What is the name of the grape used to make Merlot wine?
A) Merlot (Answer)
B) Cabernet Sauvignon

18- What is the name of the tool used to remove excess air from an open bottle of wine?
A) Wine saver (Answer)
B) Wine opener

19- What is the name of the type of wine that is made from frozen grapes?
A) Ice wine (Answer)
B) Port

20- What is the name of the region in Italy known for producing Chianti wine?
A) Tuscany (Answer)
B) Piedmont

21- What is the name of the process used to add flavor to wine by soaking wood chips in it?
A) Barrel aging
B) Oak infusion (Answer)

22- What is the name of the tool used to chill a bottle of wine quickly?
A) Wine cooler (Answer)
B) Ice bucket

23- What is the name of the grape used to make Pinot Noir wine?
A) Cabernet Sauvignon
B) Pinot Noir (Answer)

24- What is the name of the process used to make sparkling wine by inducing a secondary fermentation in the bottle?
A) Methode champenoise (Answer)
B) Carbonation

1- What is the nickname for the state of Hawaii?
A) The Aloha State
B) The Sunshine State

2- What is the capital city of Hawaii?
A) Honolulu
B) Hilo

3- What is the famous beach on the island of Oahu known for its big waves and surfing competitions?
A) Waikiki Beach
B) Pipeline Beach

4- What is the name of the active volcano on the island of Hawaii?
A) Kilauea
B) Mauna Loa

5- What is the name of the popular Hawaiian dish made with raw fish and soy sauce?
A) Poke
B) Sashimi

6- What is the name of the traditional Hawaiian dance?
A) Hula
B) Samba

7- What is the name of the famous road on the island of Maui that features 620 curves and 59 bridges?
A) The Hana Highway
B) The Road to Hilo

8- What is the name of the famous mountain on the island of Maui that is often seen with a cloud formation resembling a woman's profile?
A) Haleakala
B) Mauna Kea

9- What is the name of the famous beach on the island of Maui that is known for its black sand?
A) Wailea Beach
B) Wai'anapanapa Beach

10- What is the name of the popular Hawaiian shaved ice treat?
A) Shave Ice
B) Snow Cone

11- What is the name of the famous botanical garden on the island of Kauai?
A) Allerton Garden
B) Na 'Aina Kai Botanical Garden

12- What is the name of the famous beach on the island of Kauai that is only accessible by foot or boat?
A) Polihale Beach
B) Hanakapiai Beach

13- What is the name of the famous bay on the island of Maui that is known for its clear water and snorkeling opportunities?
A) Hana Bay
B) Honolua Bay

14- What is the name of the famous hiking trail on the island of Oahu that features steep staircases and panoramic views?
A) Diamond Head Trail
B) Koko Head Trail

15- What is the name of the famous surf spot on the island of Maui that features a giant wave known as Jaws?
A) Peahi
B) Lahaina

16- What is the name of the famous beach on the island of Kauai that is known for its red sand?
A) Poipu Beach
B) Polihale Beach

17- What is the name of the famous historical site on the island of Hawaii that was once a royal residence?
A) Pu'uhonua o Honaunau National Historical Park
B) Akaka Falls State Park

18- What is the name of the famous bay on the island of Oahu that is known for its calm waters and sea turtles?
A) Hanauma Bay
B) Waimea Bay

19- What is the name of the famous beach on the island of Maui that is known for its white sand and crystal-clear water?
A) Ka'anapali Beach
B) Napili Bay

ANSWERS:

1- What is the nickname for the state of Hawaii?
A) The Aloha State (Answer)
B) The Sunshine State

2- What is the capital city of Hawaii?
A) Honolulu (Answer)
B) Hilo

3- What is the famous beach on the island of Oahu known for its big waves and surfing competitions?
A) Waikiki Beach
B) Pipeline Beach (Answer)

4- What is the name of the active volcano on the island of Hawaii?
A) Kilauea - say "kih-luh-way-uh"" (Answer)
B) Mauna Loa

5- What is the name of the popular Hawaiian dish made with raw fish and soy sauce?
A) Poke (Answer)
B) Sashimi

6- What is the name of the traditional Hawaiian dance?
A) Hula (Answer)
B) Samba

7- What is the name of the famous road on the island of Maui that features 620 curves and 59 bridges?
A) The Hana Highway (Answer)
B) The Road to Hilo

8- What is the name of the famous mountain on the island of Maui that is often seen with a cloud formation resembling a woman's profile?
A) Haleakala (Answer)
B) Mauna Kea

9- What is the name of the famous beach on the island of Maui that is known for its black sand?
A) Wailea Beach
B) Wai'anapanapa Beach (Answer)

10- What is the name of the popular Hawaiian shaved ice treat?
A) Shave Ice (Answer)
B) Snow Cone

11- What is the name of the famous botanical garden on the island of Kauai?
A) Allerton Garden (Answer)
B) Na 'Aina Kai Botanical Garden
Kauai is pronounced as "ka-why-ee" with emphasis on the first syllable "ka".

12- What is the name of the famous beach on the island of Kauai that is only accessible by foot or boat?
A) Polihale Beach
B) Hanakapiai Beach (Answer)

13- What is the name of the famous bay on the island of Maui that is known for its clear water and snorkeling opportunities?
A) Hana Bay
B) Honolua Bay (Answer)

14- What is the name of the famous hiking trail on the island of Oahu that features steep staircases and panoramic views?
A) Diamond Head Trail (Answer)
B) Koko Head Trail

15- What is the name of the famous surf spot on the island of Maui that features a giant wave known as Jaws?
A) Peahi (Answer)
B) Lahaina

16- What is the name of the famous beach on the island of Kauai that is known for its red sand?
A) Poipu Beach
B) Polihale Beach (Answer)

17- What is the name of the famous historical site on the island of Hawaii that was once a royal residence?
A) Pu'uhonua o Honaunau National Historical Park (Answer)
B) Akaka Falls State Park

18- What is the name of the famous bay on the island of Oahu that is known for its calm waters and sea turtles?
A) Hanauma Bay (Answer)
B) Waimea Bay

19- What is the name of the famous beach on the island of Maui that is known for its white sand and crystal-clear water?
A) Ka'anapali Beach (Answer)
B) Napili Bay

1- What was Albert Einstein famous for?
A) Inventing the telephone
B) Developing the theory of relativity

2- Who wrote the Harry Potter series?
A) J.K. Rowling
B) Stephenie Meyer

3- Who was the first person to walk on the moon?
A) Neil Armstrong
B) Buzz Aldrin

4- Who painted the Mona Lisa?
A) Michelangelo
B) Leonardo da Vinci

5- Who is the lead singer of the Rolling Stones?
A) Mick Jagger
B) Paul McCartney

6- Who was the first female Prime Minister of the United Kingdom?
A) Margaret Thatcher
B) Angela Merkel

7- Who painted the Sistine Chapel?
A) Leonardo da Vinci
B) Michelangelo

8- Who wrote the novel "To Kill a Mockingbird"?
A) Harper Lee
B) Ernest Hemingway

9- Who founded Microsoft?
A) Bill Gates
B) Steve Jobs

10- Who was the first U.S. President to be impeached?
A) Richard Nixon
B) Andrew Johnson

11- Who painted "The Starry Night"?
A) Vincent van Gogh
B) Pablo Picasso

12- Who is the lead singer of the band Queen?
A) Freddie Mercury
B) Elton John

13- Who was the first woman to win a Nobel Prize?
A) Marie Curie
B) Jane Goodall

14- Who directed the movie "Jaws"?
A) Steven Spielberg
B) George Lucas

15- Who painted the "Girl with a Pearl Earring"?
A) Johannes Vermeer
B) Rembrandt van Rijn

16- Who wrote the novel "The Catcher in the Rye"?
A) J.D. Salinger
B) F. Scott Fitzgerald

17- Who was the lead guitarist of the Beatles?
A) George Harrison
B) Ringo Starr

18- Who was the first African-American President of the United States?
A) Barack Obama
B) Nelson Mandela

19- Who directed the movie "The Godfather"?
A) Francis Ford Coppola
B) Martin Scorsese

20- Who invented the telephone?
A) Alexander Graham Bell
B) Thomas Edison

21- Who painted "The Persistence of Memory"?
A) Salvador Dali
B) Claude Monet

22- Who wrote the play "Hamlet"?
A) William Shakespeare
B) Tennessee Williams

23- Who was the lead singer of the band Nirvana?
A) Kurt Cobain
B) Eddie Vedder

24- Who painted "The Birth of Venus"?
A) Sandro Botticelli
B) Leonardo da Vinci

ANSWERS

1- What was Albert Einstein famous for?
A) Inventing the telephone
B) Developing the theory of relativity (Answer)

2- Who wrote the Harry Potter series?
A) J.K. Rowling (Answer)
B) Stephenie Meyer

3- Who was the first person to walk on the moon?
A) Neil Armstrong (Answer)
B) Buzz Aldrin

4- Who painted the Mona Lisa?
A) Michelangelo
B) Leonardo da Vinci (Answer)

5- Who is the lead singer of the Rolling Stones?
A) Mick Jagger (Answer)
B) Paul McCartney

6- Who was the first female Prime Minister of the United Kingdom?
A) Margaret Thatcher (Answer)
B) Angela Merkel

7- Who painted the Sistine Chapel?
A) Leonardo da Vinci
B) Michelangelo (Answer)

8- Who wrote the novel "To Kill a Mockingbird"?
A) Harper Lee (Answer)
B) Ernest Hemingway

9- Who founded Microsoft?
A) Bill Gates (Answer)
B) Steve Jobs

10- Who was the first U.S. President to be impeached?
A) Richard Nixon
B) Andrew Johnson (Answer)

11- Who painted "The Starry Night"?
A) Vincent van Gogh (Answer)
B) Pablo Picasso

12- Who is the lead singer of the band Queen?
A) Freddie Mercury (Answer)
B) Elton John

13- Who was the first woman to win a Nobel Prize?
A) Marie Curie (Answer)
B) Jane Goodall

14- Who directed the movie "Jaws"?
A) Steven Spielberg (Answer)
B) George Lucas

15- Who painted the "Girl with a Pearl Earring"?
A) Johannes Vermeer (Answer)
B) Rembrandt van Rijn

16- Who wrote the novel "The Catcher in the Rye"?
A) J.D. Salinger (Answer)
B) F. Scott Fitzgerald

17- Who was the lead guitarist of the Beatles?
A) George Harrison (Answer)
B) Ringo Starr

18- Who was the first African-American President of the United States?
A) Barack Obama (Answer)
B) Nelson Mandela

19- Who directed the movie "The Godfather"?
A) Francis Ford Coppola (Answer)
B) Martin Scorsese

20- Who invented the telephone?
A) Alexander Graham Bell (Answer)
B) Thomas Edison

21- Who painted "The Persistence of Memory"?
A) Salvador Dali (Answer)
B) Claude Monet

22- Who wrote the play "Hamlet"?
A) William Shakespeare (Answer)
B) Tennessee Williams

23- Who was the lead singer of the band Nirvana?
A) Kurt Cobain (Answer)
B) Eddie Vedder

24- Who painted "The Birth of Venus"?
A) Sandro Botticelli (Answer)
B) Leonardo da Vinci

1- Who is credited with inventing the telephone?
A) Alexander Graham Bell
B) Thomas Edison

2- What year was the first telephone invented?
A) 1876
B) 1901

3- What was the first word spoken on the telephone?
A) "Hello"
B) "Goodbye"

4- What company was the first to mass-produce telephones?
A) AT&T
B) Verizon

5- What is the term for a device that converts sound waves into electrical signals for transmission over telephone lines?
A) Microphone
B) Speaker

6- What is the term for a device that converts electrical signals into sound waves for listening?
A) Speaker
B) Microphone

7- What is the name of the system that assigns unique telephone numbers to each phone line?
A) Telephone exchange
B) Switchboard

8- What is the area code for New York City?
A) 202
B) 212

9- What is the term for a device that allows multiple phone lines to be connected to a single telephone number?
A) Call waiting
B) Call forwarding

10- What is the term for the dialing prefix used to make long distance calls?
A) 411
B) 1

11- What is the name of the emergency phone number in the United States?
A) 999
B) 911

12- What is the term for a device that displays the phone number of an incoming call?
A) Caller ID
B) Call blocking

13- What is the term for a device that allows a telephone to be used on a computer network?
A) Modem
B) Router

14- What is the term for a phone service that allows calls to be made over the internet?
A) VoIP
B) SMS

15- What is the name of the first mobile phone?
A) Motorola DynaTAC
B) Nokia 3310

16- What is the term for a phone service that allows callers to leave recorded messages?
A) Voicemail
B) Call waiting

17- What is the name of the company that produces the iPhone?
A) Samsung
B) Apple

18- What is the term for a phone service that allows two or more people to talk simultaneously?
A) Conference call
B) Call forwarding

19- What is the term for a device that amplifies sound for those with hearing impairments?
A) Hearing aid
B) Earbuds

20- What is the name of the first phone book?
A) The Yellow Pages
B) The White Pages

21- What is the term for a device that allows a telephone to be used with a hearing aid?
A) T-coil
B) Amplifier

22- What is the name of the first person to make a phone call from a mobile phone?
A) Martin Cooper
B) Alexander Graham Bell

23- What is the term for a device that allows a telephone to be used hands-free?
A) Headset
B) Earpiece

24- What is the name of the first person to make a transatlantic telephone call?
A) Alexander Graham Bell
B) Walter Rothschild

25- What is the term for a device that allows a telephone to be used with a computer for making internet calls?
A) Softphone
B) Modem

ANSWERS

1- Who is credited with inventing the telephone?
A) Alexander Graham Bell (Answer)
B) Thomas Edison

2- What year was the first telephone invented?
A) 1876 (Answer)
B) 1901

3- What was the first word spoken on the telephone?
A) "Hello" (Answer)
B) "Goodbye"

4- What company was the first to mass-produce telephones?
A) AT&T (Answer)
B) Verizon

5- What is the term for a device that converts sound waves into electrical signals for transmission over telephone lines?
A) Microphone (Answer)
B) Speaker

6- What is the term for a device that converts electrical signals into sound waves for listening?
A) Speaker (Answer)
B) Microphone

7- What is the name of the system that assigns unique telephone numbers to each phone line?
A) Telephone exchange (Answer)
B) Switchboard

8- What is the area code for New York City?
A) 202
B) 212 (Answer)

9- What is the term for a device that allows multiple phone lines to be connected to a single telephone number?
A) Call waiting
B) Call forwarding (Answer)

10- What is the term for the dialing prefix used to make long distance calls?
A) 411
B) 1 (Answer)

11- What is the name of the emergency phone number in the United States?
A) 999
B) 911 (Answer)

12- What is the term for a device that displays the phone number of an incoming call?
A) Caller ID (Answer)
B) Call blocking

13- What is the term for a device that allows a telephone to be used on a computer network?
A) Modem (Answer)
B) Router

14- What is the term for a phone service that allows calls to be made over the internet?
A) VoIP (Answer)
B) SMS

15- What is the name of the first mobile phone?
A) Motorola DynaTAC (Answer)
B) Nokia 3310

16- What is the term for a phone service that allows callers to leave recorded messages?
A) Voicemail (Answer)
B) Call waiting

17- What is the name of the company that produces the iPhone?
A) Samsung
B) Apple (Answer)

18- What is the term for a phone service that allows two or more people to talk simultaneously?
A) Conference call (Answer)
B) Call forwarding

19- What is the term for a device that amplifies sound for those with hearing impairments?
A) Hearing aid (Answer)
B) Earbuds

20- What is the name of the first phone book?
A) The Yellow Pages
B) The White Pages (Answer)

21- What is the term for a device that allows a telephone to be used with a hearing aid?
A) T-coil (Answer)
B) Amplifier

22- What is the name of the first person to make a phone call from a mobile phone?
A) Martin Cooper (Answer)
B) Alexander Graham Bell

23- What is the term for a device that allows a telephone to be used hands-free?
A) Headset (Answer)
B) Earpiece

24- What is the name of the first person to make a transatlantic telephone call?
A) Alexander Graham Bell
B) Walter Rothschild (Answer)

25- What is the term for a device that allows a telephone to be used with a computer for making internet calls?
A) Softphone (Answer)
B) Modem

1- What is the name of the classic board game where players move their pieces around the board and try to get all their pieces "home"?
A) Sorry!
B) Parcheesi

2- What is the name of the board game that features colorful candy-like pieces and a winding, rainbow-colored track?
A) Chutes and Ladders
B) Candyland

3- What is the name of the classic strategy game where players capture each other's pieces by jumping over them?
A) Checkers
B) Tic Tac Toe

4- What is the name of the board game that challenges players to create as many words as possible from a set of letter tiles?
A) Scrabble
B) Boggle

5- What is the name of the board game that features a plastic pop-o-matic die roller and encourages players to get all their pieces to the finish line first?
A) Trouble
B) Snakes and Ladders

6- What is the name of the board game where players try to guess the identity of their opponent's "secret" character?
A) Guess Who?
B) Clue

7- What is the name of the board game that features a 10x10 grid and different pieces that can move in different ways to capture their opponents?
A) Chess
B) Connect Four

8- What is the name of the board game that challenges players to build and manage their own railway empire?
A) Monopoly
B) Ticket to Ride

9- What is the name of the board game that features different colored properties and encourages players to buy and sell them to become the wealthiest player?
A) Life
B) Monopoly

10- What is the name of the board game that features tiles with different terrain types and allows players to build and expand their own kingdom?
A) Carcassonne
B) Settlers of Catan

11- What is the name of the board game that features a vertical board with rows of sliding tiles and encourages players to line up their pieces in a row of four?
A) Connect Four
B) Quarto

12- What is the name of the board game that challenges players to navigate through a maze and collect treasure while avoiding traps and monsters?
A) Dungeon
B) Labyrinth

13- What is the name of the board game that challenges players to solve a murder mystery by collecting clues and eliminating suspects?
A) Clue
B) Guess Who?

14- What is the name of the board game that challenges players to build and expand their own city by placing tiles and claiming resources?
A) Settlers of Catan
B) Risk

15- What is the name of the board game that features different categories of questions and challenges players to move their pieces around the board by answering them correctly?
A) Trivial Pursuit
B) Scattergories

16- What is the name of the board game that challenges players to bluff and outwit their opponents to become the last player standing?
A) Poker
B) Sheriff of Nottingham

17- What is the name of the board game that challenges players to build and manage their own amusement park?
A) Roller Coaster Tycoon
B) Theme Park

18- What is the name of the board game that challenges players to build and expand their own farm by planting crops and raising animals?
A) Agricola
B) Club

ANSWERS

1- What is the name of the classic board game where players move their pieces around the board and try to get all their pieces "home"?
A) Sorry!
B) Parcheesi (Answer)

2- What is the name of the board game that features colorful candy-like pieces and a winding, rainbow-colored track?
A) Chutes and Ladders
B) Candyland (Answer)

3- What is the name of the classic strategy game where players capture each other's pieces by jumping over them?
A) Checkers (Answer)
B) Tic Tac Toe

4- What is the name of the board game that challenges players to create as many words as possible from a set of letter tiles?
A) Scrabble (Answer)
B) Boggle

5- What is the name of the board game that features a plastic pop-o-matic die roller and encourages players to get all their pieces to the finish line first?
A) Trouble (Answer)
B) Snakes and Ladders

6- What is the name of the board game where players try to guess the identity of their opponent's "secret" character?
A) Guess Who? (Answer)
B) Clue

7- What is the name of the board game that features a 10x10 grid and different pieces that can move in different ways to capture their opponents?
A) Chess (Answer)
B) Connect Four

8- What is the name of the board game that challenges players to build and manage their own railway empire?
A) Monopoly
B) Ticket to Ride (Answer)

9- What is the name of the board game that features different colored properties and encourages players to buy and sell them to become the wealthiest player?
A) Life
B) Monopoly (Answer)

10- What is the name of the board game that features tiles with different terrain types and allows players to build and expand their own kingdom?
A) Carcassonne (Answer)
B) Settlers of Catan

11- What is the name of the board game that features a vertical board with rows of sliding tiles and encourages players to line up their pieces in a row of four?
A) Connect Four
B) Quarto (Answer)

12- What is the name of the board game that challenges players to navigate through a maze and collect treasure while avoiding traps and monsters?
A) Dungeon
B) Labyrinth (Answer)

13- What is the name of the board game that challenges players to solve a murder mystery by collecting clues and eliminating suspects?
A) Clue (Answer)
B) Guess Who?

14- What is the name of the board game that challenges players to build and expand their own city by placing tiles and claiming resources?
A) Settlers of Catan (Answer)
B) Risk

15- What is the name of the board game that features different categories of questions and challenges players to move their pieces around the board by answering them correctly?
A) Trivial Pursuit (Answer)
B) Scattergories

16- What is the name of the board game that challenges players to bluff and outwit their opponents to become the last player standing?
A) Poker
B) Sheriff of Nottingham (Answer)

17- What is the name of the board game that challenges players to build and manage their own amusement park?
A) Roller Coaster Tycoon
B) Theme Park (Answer)

18- What is the name of the board game that challenges players to build and expand their own farm by planting crops and raising animals?
A) Agricola (Answer)
B) Club

1- How many innings are there in a regulation game of baseball?
A) Nine innings
B) Seven innings

2- Who is the all-time home run leader in Major League Baseball?
A) Barry Bonds
B) Babe Ruth

3- What is the term for when a batter hits the ball and reaches first base safely without getting out?
A) Single
B) Out

4- Who is the only pitcher in Major League Baseball history to throw a perfect game in the World Series?
A) Don Larsen
B) Sandy Koufax

5- Which team has won the most World Series championships?
A) New York Yankees
B) Los Angeles Dodgers

6- Who was the first African American player in Major League Baseball?
A) Jackie Robinson
B) Willie Mays

7- How many strikes are needed to strike out a batter in baseball?
A) Three strikes
B) Four strikes

8- Which team holds the record for the longest winning streak in Major League Baseball history?
A) Cleveland Indians
B) New York Yankees

9- Who is the only player to hit two grand slams in a single inning?
A) Fernando Tatis
B) Hank Aaron

10- What is the term for when a pitcher throws three strikes to a batter?
A) Strikeout
B) Homerun

11- Which player holds the record for the most stolen bases in a season?
A) Rickey Henderson
B) Babe Ruth

12- Which player holds the record for the most career hits in Major League Baseball?
A) Pete Rose
B) Ty Cobb

13- Which team did Babe Ruth play for before joining the New York Yankees?
A) Boston Red Sox
B) St. Louis Cardinals

14- Which pitcher holds the record for the most career strikeouts?
A) Nolan Ryan
B) Roger Clemens

15- Who was the first player to hit 500 career home runs in Major League Baseball?
A) Babe Ruth
B) Hank Aaron

16- Which team did Joe DiMaggio play for during his entire career?
A) New York Yankees
B) Boston Red Sox

17- What is the term for when a batter hits the ball out of the playing field for a home run?
A) Home Run
B) Strikeout

18- Who was the first pitcher to win 300 games in Major League Baseball?
A) Cy Young
B) Sandy Koufax

19- Which player holds the record for the most home runs in a single season?
A) Barry Bonds
B) Mark McGwire

20- Who holds the record for the most consecutive games with a hit in Major League Baseball?
A) Joe DiMaggio
B) Pete Rose

21- Which pitcher holds the record for the most career wins?
A) Cy Young
B) Randy Johnson

22- Who is the only player in Major League Baseball history to win the Most Valuable Player award unanimously?
A) Ken Griffey Jr.
B) Barry Bonds

23- Which team did Willie Mays play for during his entire career?
A) New York Giants/San Francisco Giants
B) Los Angeles Dodgers

24- Which player holds the record for the most career RBIs in Major League Baseball?
A) Hank Aaron
B) Alex Rodriguez

ANSWERS

1- How many innings are there in a regulation game of baseball?
A) Nine innings (Answer)
B) Seven innings

2- Who is the all-time home run leader in Major League Baseball?
A) Barry Bonds (Answer)
B) Babe Ruth

3- What is the term for when a batter hits the ball and reaches first base safely without getting out?
A) Single (Answer)
B) Out

4- Who is the only pitcher in Major League Baseball history to throw a perfect game in the World Series?
A) Don Larsen (Answer)
B) Sandy Koufax

5- Which team has won the most World Series championships?
A) New York Yankees (Answer)
B) Los Angeles Dodgers

6- Who was the first African American player in Major League Baseball?
A) Jackie Robinson (Answer)
B) Willie Mays

7- How many strikes are needed to strike out a batter in baseball?
A) Three strikes (Answer)
B) Four strikes

8- Which team holds the record for the longest winning streak in Major League Baseball history?
A) Cleveland Indians (Answer)
B) New York Yankees

9- Who is the only player to hit two grand slams in a single inning?
A) Fernando Tatis (Answer)
B) Hank Aaron

10- What is the term for when a pitcher throws three strikes to a batter?
A) Strikeout (Answer)
B) Homerun

11- Which player holds the record for the most stolen bases in a season?
A) Rickey Henderson (Answer)
B) Babe Ruth

12- Which player holds the record for the most career hits in Major League Baseball?
A) Pete Rose (Answer)
B) Ty Cobb

13- Which team did Babe Ruth play for before joining the New York Yankees?
A) Boston Red Sox (Answer)
B) St. Louis Cardinals

14- Which pitcher holds the record for the most career strikeouts?
A) Nolan Ryan (Answer)
B) Roger Clemens

15- Who was the first player to hit 500 career home runs in Major League Baseball?
A) Babe Ruth (Answer)
B) Hank Aaron

16- Which team did Joe DiMaggio play for during his entire career?
A) New York Yankees (Answer)
B) Boston Red Sox

17- What is the term for when a batter hits the ball out of the playing field for a home run?
A) Home Run (Answer)
B) Strikeout

18- Who was the first pitcher to win 300 games in Major League Baseball?
A) Cy Young (Answer)
B) Sandy Koufax

19- Which player holds the record for the most home runs in a single season?
A) Barry Bonds (Answer)
B) Mark McGwire

20- Who holds the record for the most consecutive games with a hit in Major League Baseball?
A) Joe DiMaggio (Answer)
B) Pete Rose

21- Which pitcher holds the record for the most career wins?
A) Cy Young (Answer)
B) Randy Johnson

22- Who is the only player in Major League Baseball history to win the Most Valuable Player award unanimously?
A) Ken Griffey Jr. (Answer)
B) Barry Bonds

23- Which team did Willie Mays play for during his entire career?
A) New York Giants/San Francisco Giants (Answer)
B) Los Angeles Dodgers

24- Which player holds the record for the most career RBIs in Major League Baseball?
A) Hank Aaron (Answer)
B) Alex Rodriguez

1- What is the name of the device that helps an airplane change altitude?
A) Elevator
B) Rudder

2- What is the name of the part of the airplane that controls the pitch?
A) Stabilizer
B) Winglet

3- What is the name of the device that helps an airplane turn?
A) Aileron
B) Flap

4- What is the name of the device that helps slow down the airplane during landing?
A) Flap
B) Spoiler

5- What is the name of the device that helps the airplane steer on the ground?
A) Nose wheel
B) Tail wheel

6- What is the name of the part of the airplane that generates lift?
A) Wing
B) Tail

7- What is the name of the device that helps an airplane climb?
A) Thrust
B) Flap

8- What is the name of the device that helps an airplane brake during landing?
A) Spoiler
B) Flap

9- What is the name of the part of the airplane that houses the passengers and crew?
A) Fuselage
B) Cockpit

10- What is the name of the device that helps an airplane stabilize during flight?
A) Horizontal stabilizer
B) Vertical stabilizer

11- What is the name of the device that helps an airplane take off?
A) Thrust
B) Flap

12- What is the name of the part of the airplane that contains the engines?
A) Wing
B) Nacelle

13- What is the name of the device that helps an airplane maintain altitude?
A) Trim tab
B) Spoiler

14- What is the name of the device that helps an airplane fly in a straight line?
A) Rudder
B) Aileron

15- What is the name of the part of the airplane that attaches the wings to the fuselage?
A) Wing strut
B) Winglet

16- What is the name of the device that helps an airplane reduce drag during flight?
A) Winglet
B) Flap

17- What is the name of the device that helps an airplane reduce turbulence during flight?
A) Winglet
B) Spoiler

18- What is the name of the device that helps an airplane reduce noise during flight?
A) Hush kit
B) Thrust reverser

19- What is the name of the part of the airplane that houses the landing gear?
A) Fuselage
B) Landing gear compartment

20- What is the name of the device that helps an airplane increase lift during takeoff?
A) Flap
B) Spoiler

21- What is the name of the device that helps an airplane reduce speed during landing?
A) Spoiler
B) Flap

22- What is the name of the part of the airplane that connects the wings to the fuselage?
A) Wing root
B) Winglet

23- What is the name of the device that helps an airplane control its yaw?
A) Rudder
B) Aileron

24- What is the name of the device that helps an airplane slow down during landing without using the brakes?
A) Thrust reverser
B) Ion Thruster

ANSWERS

1- What is the name of the device that helps an airplane change altitude?
A) Elevator (Answer)
B) Rudder

2- What is the name of the part of the airplane that controls the pitch?
A) Stabilizer (Answer)
B) Winglet

3- What is the name of the device that helps an airplane turn?
A) Aileron (Answer)
B) Flap

4- What is the name of the device that helps slow down the airplane during landing?
A) Flap (Answer)
B) Spoiler

5- What is the name of the device that helps the airplane steer on the ground?
A) Nose wheel (Answer)
B) Tail wheel

6- What is the name of the part of the airplane that generates lift?
A) Wing (Answer)
B) Tail

7- What is the name of the device that helps an airplane climb?
A) Thrust (Answer)
B) Flap

8- What is the name of the device that helps an airplane brake during landing?
A) Spoiler (Answer)
B) Flap

9- What is the name of the part of the airplane that houses the passengers and crew?
A) Fuselage (Answer)
B) Cockpit

10- What is the name of the device that helps an airplane stabilize during flight?
A) Horizontal stabilizer (Answer)
B) Vertical stabilizer

11- What is the name of the device that helps an airplane take off?
A) Thrust (Answer)
B) Flap

12- What is the name of the part of the airplane that contains the engines?
A) Wing
B) Nacelle (Answer)

13- What is the name of the device that helps an airplane maintain altitude?
A) Trim tab (Answer)
B) Spoiler

14- What is the name of the device that helps an airplane fly in a straight line?
A) Rudder
B) Aileron (Answer)

15- What is the name of the part of the airplane that attaches the wings to the fuselage?
A) Wing strut (Answer)
B) Winglet

16- What is the name of the device that helps an airplane reduce drag during flight?
A) Winglet (Answer)
B) Flap

17- What is the name of the device that helps an airplane reduce turbulence during flight?
A) Winglet (Answer)
B) Spoiler

18- What is the name of the device that helps an airplane reduce noise during flight?
A) Hush kit (Answer)
B) Thrust reverser

19- What is the name of the part of the airplane that houses the landing gear?
A) Fuselage
B) Landing gear compartment (Answer)

20- What is the name of the device that helps an airplane increase lift during takeoff?
A) Flap (Answer)
B) Spoiler

21- What is the name of the device that helps an airplane reduce speed during landing?
A) Spoiler (Answer)
B) Flap

22- What is the name of the part of the airplane that connects the wings to the fuselage?
A) Wing root (Answer)
B) Winglet

23- What is the name of the device that helps an airplane control its yaw?
A) Rudder (Answer)
B) Aileron

24- What is the name of the device that helps an airplane slow down during landing without using the brakes?
A) Thrust reverser (Answer)
B) Ion Thruster

1- Who is the author of the Harry Potter book series?
A) J.K. Rowling
B) Stephen King

2- Who wrote the bestselling novel "The Da Vinci Code"?
A) Dan Brown
B) John Grisham

3- Who wrote the classic novel "To Kill a Mockingbird"?
A) Harper Lee
B) Jane Austen

4- Who is the author of the "Twilight" book series?
A) Stephenie Meyer
B) Suzanne Collins

5- Who wrote the bestselling book "The Hunger Games"?
A) Suzanne Collins
B) Veronica Roth

6- Who is the author of the bestselling book series "A Song of Ice and Fire"?
A) George R.R. Martin
B) J.R.R. Tolkien

7- Who wrote the bestselling novel "Gone Girl"?
A) Gillian Flynn
B) Paula Hawkins

8- Who is the author of the bestselling book "The Girl with the Dragon Tattoo"?
A) Stieg Larsson
B) David Baldacci

9- Who wrote the bestselling novel "The Fault in Our Stars"?
A) John Green
B) Nicholas Sparks

10- Who is the author of the bestselling book "The Alchemist"?
A) Paulo Coelho
B) Gabriel Garcia Marquez

11- Who wrote the bestselling novel "The Girl on the Train"?
A) Paula Hawkins
B) Gillian Flynn

12- Who is the author of the bestselling book "The Kite Runner"?
A) Khaled Hosseini
B) Jhumpa Lahiri

13- Who wrote the bestselling novel "The Help"?
A) Kathryn Stockett
B) Jodi Picoult

14- Who is the author of the bestselling book "The Chronicles of Narnia"?
A) C.S. Lewis
B) J.K. Rowling

15- Who wrote the bestselling novel "The Bridges of Madison County"?
A) Robert James Waller
B) Nicholas Sparks

16- Who is the author of the bestselling book "The Catcher in the Rye"?
A) J.D. Salinger
B) Ernest Hemingway

17- Who wrote the bestselling book "The Lovely Bones"?
A) Alice Sebold
B) Donna Tartt

18- Who is the author of the bestselling book "The Adventures of Huckleberry Finn"?
A) Mark Twain
B) Edgar Allan Poe

19- Who wrote the bestselling novel "The Notebook"?
A) Nicholas Sparks
B) John Green

20- Who is the author of the bestselling book "One Hundred Years of Solitude"?
A) Gabriel Garcia Marquez
B) Isabel Allende

21- Who wrote the bestselling novel "The Help"?
A) Kathryn Stockett
B) Jodi Picoult

22- Who is the author of the bestselling book "The Picture of Dorian Gray"?
A) Oscar Wilde
B) Virginia Woolf

23- Who wrote the bestselling novel "The Lord of the Rings"?
A) J.R.R. Tolkien
B) George R.R. Martin

ANSWERS

1- Who is the author of the Harry Potter book series?
A) J.K. Rowling (Answer)
B) Stephen King

2- Who wrote the bestselling novel "The Da Vinci Code"?
A) Dan Brown (Answer)
B) John Grisham

3- Who wrote the classic novel "To Kill a Mockingbird"?
A) Harper Lee (Answer)
B) Jane Austen

4- Who is the author of the "Twilight" book series?
A) Stephenie Meyer (Answer)
B) Suzanne Collins

5- Who wrote the bestselling book "The Hunger Games"?
A) Suzanne Collins (Answer)
B) Veronica Roth

6- Who is the author of the bestselling book series "A Song of Ice and Fire"?
A) George R.R. Martin (Answer)
B) J.R.R. Tolkien

7- Who wrote the bestselling novel "Gone Girl"?
A) Gillian Flynn (Answer)
B) Paula Hawkins

8- Who is the author of the bestselling book "The Girl with the Dragon Tattoo"?
A) Stieg Larsson (Answer)
B) David Baldacci

9- Who wrote the bestselling novel "The Fault in Our Stars"?
A) John Green (Answer)
B) Nicholas Sparks

10- Who is the author of the bestselling book "The Alchemist"?
A) Paulo Coelho (Answer)
B) Gabriel Garcia Marquez

11- Who wrote the bestselling novel "The Girl on the Train"?
A) Paula Hawkins (Answer)
B) Gillian Flynn

12- Who is the author of the bestselling book "The Kite Runner"?
A) Khaled Hosseini (Answer)
B) Jhumpa Lahiri

13- Who wrote the bestselling novel "The Help"?
A) Kathryn Stockett (Answer)
B) Jodi Picoult

14- Who is the author of the bestselling book "The Chronicles of Narnia"?
A) C.S. Lewis (Answer)
B) J.K. Rowling

15- Who wrote the bestselling novel "The Bridges of Madison County"?
A) Robert James Waller (Answer)
B) Nicholas Sparks

16- Who is the author of the bestselling book "The Catcher in the Rye"?
A) J.D. Salinger (Answer)
B) Ernest Hemingway

17- Who wrote the bestselling book "The Lovely Bones"?
A) Alice Sebold (Answer)
B) Donna Tartt

18- Who is the author of the bestselling book "The Adventures of Huckleberry Finn"?
A) Mark Twain (Answer)
B) Edgar Allan Poe

19- Who wrote the bestselling novel "The Notebook"?
A) Nicholas Sparks (Answer)
B) John Green

20- Who is the author of the bestselling book "One Hundred Years of Solitude"?
A) Gabriel Garcia Marquez (Answer)
B) Isabel Allende

21- Who wrote the bestselling novel "The Help"?
A) Kathryn Stockett (Answer)
B) Jodi Picoult

22- Who is the author of the bestselling book "The Picture of Dorian Gray"?
A) Oscar Wilde (Answer)
B) Virginia Woolf

23- Who wrote the bestselling novel "The Lord of the Rings"?
A) J.R.R. Tolkien (Answer)
B) George R.R. Martin

1- What is the art of folding paper to create decorative objects called?
A) Origami
B) Knitting

2- What type of paint is made by mixing pigment with egg yolk?
A) Tempera
B) Oil paint

3- What type of needlework uses a hook to create interlocking loops of yarn or thread?
A) Crochet
B) Cross-stitch

4- Which type of paint uses water-soluble pigments and is typically used on paper or canvas?
A) Watercolor
B) Acrylic

5- What is the Japanese art of repairing broken pottery with gold called?
A) Kintsugi
B) Calligraphy

6- Which type of paper-folding originated in Germany and involves folding and cutting paper to create intricate designs?
A) Scherenschnitte
B) Kirigami

7- What is the process of dying fabric by tying it in certain areas called?
A) Tie-dyeing
B) Batik

8- Which type of art involves creating three-dimensional objects out of materials such as clay, wood, or stone?
A) Sculpture
B) Painting

9- What is the technique of printing using a raised surface called?
A) Relief printing
B) Screen printing

10- Which type of needlework uses a needle and thread to create a picture or design on fabric?
A) Embroidery
B) Knitting

11- Which type of art involves creating images using a pen or pencil on paper?
A) Drawing
B) Painting

12- What is the technique of making prints by carving a design into a woodblock called?
A) Woodcut
B) Etching

13- Which type of paint is made by mixing pigment with melted wax?
A) Encaustic
B) Watercolor

14- What is the technique of creating a design by arranging small pieces of colored glass or stone called?
A) Mosaic
B) Collage

15- Which type of needlework involves using a needle to create a series of stitches on fabric, typically in a repetitive pattern?
A) Cross-stitch
B) Crochet

16- Which type of art involves creating designs or images by cutting out paper shapes and gluing them onto a surface?
A) Collage
B) Decoupage

17- What is the art of making objects by shaping and joining pieces of wood called?
A) Woodworking
B) Pottery

18- Which type of paint uses pigment mixed with egg yolk and vinegar?
A) Egg tempera
B) Oil paint

19- What is the technique of creating a design by weaving colored threads or yarn together called?
A) Tapestry
B) Macrame

20- Which type of art involves creating images by arranging and gluing small pieces of paper or other materials onto a surface?
A) Collage
B) Mosaic

21- What is the technique of printing using a stencil called?
A) Screen printing
B) Relief printing

22- Which type of art involves creating images by pressing ink onto a surface using a raised design?
A) Letterpress
B) Linocut

23- What is the process of creating designs by cutting away parts of a surface using a sharp tool called?
A) Engraving
B) Grading

ANSWERS

1- What is the art of folding paper to create decorative objects called?
A) Origami (Answer)
B) Knitting

2- What type of paint is made by mixing pigment with egg yolk?
A) Tempera (Answer)
B) Oil paint

3- What type of needlework uses a hook to create interlocking loops of yarn or thread?
A) Crochet (Answer)
B) Cross-stitch

4- Which type of paint uses water-soluble pigments and is typically used on paper or canvas?
A) Watercolor (Answer)
B) Acrylic

5- What is the Japanese art of repairing broken pottery with gold called?
A) Kintsugi (Answer)
B) Calligraphy

6- Which type of paper-folding originated in Germany and involves folding and cutting paper to create intricate designs?
A) Scherenschnitte (Answer)
B) Kirigami

7- What is the process of dying fabric by tying it in certain areas called?
A) Tie-dyeing (Answer)
B) Batik

8- Which type of art involves creating three-dimensional objects out of materials such as clay, wood, or stone?
A) Sculpture (Answer)
B) Painting

9- What is the technique of printing using a raised surface called?
A) Relief printing (Answer)
B) Screen printing

10- Which type of needlework uses a needle and thread to create a picture or design on fabric?
A) Embroidery (Answer)
B) Knitting

11- Which type of art involves creating images using a pen or pencil on paper?
A) Drawing (Answer)
B) Painting

12- What is the technique of making prints by carving a design into a woodblock called?
A) Woodcut (Answer)
B) Etching

13- Which type of paint is made by mixing pigment with melted wax?
A) Encaustic (Answer)
B) Watercolor

14- What is the technique of creating a design by arranging small pieces of colored glass or stone called?
A) Mosaic (Answer)
B) Collage

15- Which type of needlework involves using a needle to create a series of stitches on fabric, typically in a repetitive pattern?
A) Cross-stitch (Answer)
B) Crochet

16- Which type of art involves creating designs or images by cutting out paper shapes and gluing them onto a surface?
A) Collage (Answer)
B) Decoupage

17- What is the art of making objects by shaping and joining pieces of wood called?
A) Woodworking (Answer)
B) Pottery

18- Which type of paint uses pigment mixed with egg yolk and vinegar?
A) Egg tempera (Answer)
B) Oil paint

19- What is the technique of creating a design by weaving colored threads or yarn together called?
A) Tapestry (Answer)
B) Macrame

20- Which type of art involves creating images by arranging and gluing small pieces of paper or other materials onto a surface?
A) Collage (Answer)
B) Mosaic

21- What is the technique of printing using a stencil called?
A) Screen printing (Answer)
B) Relief printing

22- Which type of art involves creating images by pressing ink onto a surface using a raised design?
A) Letterpress (Answer)
B) Linocut

23- What is the process of creating designs by cutting away parts of a surface using a sharp tool called?
A) Engraving (Answer)
B) Grading

1- What is the name of the insect that is known for its bright green color and is often used as a symbol of good luck?
A) Grasshopper
B) Praying Mantis

2- What is the name of the insect that is known for its painful sting and aggressive behavior?
A) Honeybee
B) Yellowjacket

3- What is the name of the insect that is known for its ability to jump great distances?
A) Ant
B) Grasshopper

4- What is the name of the insect that is known for its ability to camouflage itself to look like a stick or a leaf?
A) Ladybug
B) Walking Stick

5- What is the name of the insect that is known for its loud buzzing sound and ability to sting multiple times?
A) Honeybee
B) Wasp

6- What is the name of the insect that is known for its ability to carry 50 times its own body weight?
A) Ant
B) Ladybug

7- What is the name of the insect that is known for its hard shell and ability to play dead when threatened?
A) Cockroach
B) Beetle

8- What is the name of the insect that is known for its colorful wings and ability to fly long distances?
A) Butterfly
B) Moth

9- What is the name of the insect that is known for its ability to spin webs and capture prey?
A) Spider
B) Ant

10- What is the name of the insect that is known for its ability to carry diseases and transmit them to humans?
A) Ladybug
B) Mosquito

11- What is the name of the insect that is known for its social behavior and ability to work together in large colonies?
A) Butterfly
B) Ant

12- What is the name of the insect that is known for its bright colors and ability to warn predators with its toxicity?
A) Ladybug
B) Poison Dart Frog

13- What is the name of the insect that is known for its hard exoskeleton and ability to curl up into a ball when threatened?
A) Armadillo
B) Pill Bug

14- What is the name of the insect that is known for its ability to mimic the appearance of a bee or wasp to deter predators?
A) Fly
B) Hoverfly

15- What is the name of the insect that is known for its ability to navigate using the position of the sun and stars?
A) Butterfly
B) Bee

16- What is the name of the insect that is known for its long, thin body and ability to move silently?
A) Grasshopper
B) Praying Mantis

17- What is the name of the insect that is known for its ability to swarm and devour crops?
A) Ladybug
B) Locust

18- What is the name of the insect that is known for its ability to produce silk and spin webs?
A) Ant
B) Spider

19- What is the name of the insect that is known for its ability to jump great distances and communicate with vibrations?
A) Flea
B) Cricket

20- What is the name of the insect that is known for its ability to burrow and tunnel underground?
A) Beetle
B) Ant

ANSWERS

1- What is the name of the insect that is known for its bright green color and is often used as a symbol of good luck?
A) Grasshopper
B) Praying Mantis (Answer)

2- What is the name of the insect that is known for its painful sting and aggressive behavior?
A) Honeybee
B) Yellowjacket (Answer)

3- What is the name of the insect that is known for its ability to jump great distances?
A) Ant
B) Grasshopper (Answer)

4- What is the name of the insect that is known for its ability to camouflage itself to look like a stick or a leaf?
A) Ladybug
B) Walking Stick (Answer)

5- What is the name of the insect that is known for its loud buzzing sound and ability to sting multiple times?
A) Honeybee
B) Wasp (Answer)

6- What is the name of the insect that is known for its ability to carry 50 times its own body weight?
A) Ant (Answer)
B) Ladybug

7- What is the name of the insect that is known for its hard shell and ability to play dead when threatened?
A) Cockroach
B) Beetle (Answer)

8- What is the name of the insect that is known for its colorful wings and ability to fly long distances?
A) Butterfly (Answer)
B) Moth

9- What is the name of the insect that is known for its ability to spin webs and capture prey?
A) Spider (Answer)
B) Ant

10- What is the name of the insect that is known for its ability to carry diseases and transmit them to humans?
A) Ladybug
B) Mosquito (Answer)

11- What is the name of the insect that is known for its social behavior and ability to work together in large colonies?
A) Butterfly
B) Ant (Answer)

12- What is the name of the insect that is known for its bright colors and ability to warn predators with its toxicity?
A) Ladybug
B) Poison Dart Frog (Answer)

13- What is the name of the insect that is known for its hard exoskeleton and ability to curl up into a ball when threatened?
A) Armadillo
B) Pill Bug (Answer)

14- What is the name of the insect that is known for its ability to mimic the appearance of a bee or wasp to deter predators?
A) Fly
B) Hoverfly (Answer)

15- What is the name of the insect that is known for its ability to navigate using the position of the sun and stars?
A) Butterfly
B) Bee (Answer)

16- What is the name of the insect that is known for its long, thin body and ability to move silently?
A) Grasshopper
B) Praying Mantis

17- What is the name of the insect that is known for its ability to swarm and devour crops?
A) Ladybug
B) Locust (Answer)

18- What is the name of the insect that is known for its ability to produce silk and spin webs?
A) Ant
B) Spider (Answer)

19- What is the name of the insect that is known for its ability to jump great distances and communicate with vibrations?
A) Flea
B) Cricket (Answer)

20- What is the name of the insect that is known for its ability to burrow and tunnel underground?
A) Beetle
B) Ant (Answer)

1- What is the name of the famous building block toy that has been around since the 1930s?
A) Lego
B) Duplo

2- What is the name of the famous doll that was first introduced in 1959?
A) Barbie
B) Bratz

3- What is the name of the famous toy car that was introduced in the 1960s?
A) Hot Wheels
B) Matchbox

4- What is the name of the famous board game that involves buying and selling properties?
A) Monopoly
B) Scrabble

5- What is the name of the famous electronic pet that was popular in the late 1990s?
A) Tamagotchi
B) Furby

6- What is the name of the famous construction toy that consists of colorful interlocking plastic bricks?
A) Lego
B) K'NEX

7- What is the name of the famous action figure that was first introduced in the 1960s?
A) G.I. Joe
B) He-Man

8- What is the name of the famous plush toy that was first introduced in the 1980s?
A) Care Bears
B) Trolls

9- What is the name of the famous building toy that uses magnetic pieces?
A) Magformers
B) Tinkertoys

10- What is the name of the famous toy that consists of a spinning top and a string?
A) Yo-yo
B) Spinning Top

11- What is the name of the famous toy that involves creating designs with small plastic beads?
A) Perler Beads
B) Shrinky Dinks

12- What is the name of the famous toy that involves balancing a tower of blocks and removing them one by one?
A) Jenga
B) Connect Four

13- What is the name of the famous toy that involves a plastic disc being thrown and caught?
A) Frisbee
B) Hula Hoop

14- What is the name of the famous toy that involves a rubber ball being bounced against a wall?
A) Handball
B) Four Square

15- What is the name of the famous toy that involves manipulating a string to make different shapes?
A) Yo-yo
B) Kendama

16- What is the name of the famous toy that involves spinning a plastic top and trying to keep it spinning?
A) Beyblade
B) Pog

17- What is the name of the famous toy that involves a board with holes and pegs being moved around to solve a puzzle?
A) Solitaire
B) Chinese Checkers

18- What is the name of the famous toy that involves twisting and manipulating a cube to match different patterns?
A) Rubik's Cube
B) Sudoku Cube

19- What is the name of the famous toy that involves throwing and catching a boomerang-shaped object?
A) Boomerang
B) Aerobie

20- What is the name of the famous toy that involves a small ball being bounced and caught in a cup attached to a handle?
A) Ball-in-a-Cup
B) Kendama

ANSWERS

1- What is the name of the famous building block toy that has been around since the 1930s?
A) Lego (Answer)
B) Duplo

2- What is the name of the famous doll that was first introduced in 1959?
A) Barbie (Answer)
B) Bratz

3- What is the name of the famous toy car that was introduced in the 1960s?
A) Hot Wheels (Answer)
B) Matchbox

4- What is the name of the famous board game that involves buying and selling properties?
A) Monopoly (Answer)
B) Scrabble

5- What is the name of the famous electronic pet that was popular in the late 1990s?
A) Tamagotchi (Answer)
B) Furby

6- What is the name of the famous construction toy that consists of colorful interlocking plastic bricks?
A) Lego (Answer)
B) K'NEX

7- What is the name of the famous action figure that was first introduced in the 1960s?
A) G.I. Joe (Answer)
B) He-Man

8- What is the name of the famous plush toy that was first introduced in the 1980s?
A) Care Bears (Answer)
B) Trolls

9- What is the name of the famous building toy that uses magnetic pieces?
A) Magformers (Answer)
B) Tinkertoys

10- What is the name of the famous toy that consists of a spinning top and a string?
A) Yo-yo (Answer)
B) Spinning Top

11- What is the name of the famous toy that involves creating designs with small plastic beads?
A) Perler Beads (Answer)
B) Shrinky Dinks

12- What is the name of the famous toy that involves balancing a tower of blocks and removing them one by one?
A) Jenga (Answer)
B) Connect Four

13- What is the name of the famous toy that involves a plastic disc being thrown and caught?
A) Frisbee (Answer)
B) Hula Hoop

14- What is the name of the famous toy that involves a rubber ball being bounced against a wall?
A) Handball (Answer)
B) Four Square

15- What is the name of the famous toy that involves manipulating a string to make different shapes?
A) Yo-yo (Answer)
B) Kendama

16- What is the name of the famous toy that involves spinning a plastic top and trying to keep it spinning?
A) Beyblade (Answer)
B) Pog

17- What is the name of the famous toy that involves a board with holes and pegs being moved around to solve a puzzle?
A) Solitaire (Answer)
B) Chinese Checkers

18- What is the name of the famous toy that involves twisting and manipulating a cube to match different patterns?
A) Rubik's Cube (Answer)
B) Sudoku Cube

19- What is the name of the famous toy that involves throwing and catching a boomerang-shaped object?
A) Boomerang (Answer)
B) Aerobie

20- What is the name of the famous toy that involves a small ball being bounced and caught in a cup attached to a handle?
A) Ball-in-a-Cup (Answer)
B) Kendama

1- What candy bar is made with nougat, caramel, and peanuts?
A) Snickers B) Butterfinger

2- What candy is shaped like a bottle and has a cola flavor?
A) Cola Bottles B) Gummy Bears

3- What candy brand makes "Fun Dip"?
A) Wonka B) Reese's

4- What candy is shaped like a small ball and has a hard outer shell with a chewy center?
A) Jawbreakers B) M&Ms

5- What candy is a combination of chocolate, caramel, and nougat?
A) Milky Way B) Twix

6- What candy is shaped like a small fish and has a fruity flavor?
A) Swedish Fish B) Gummi Bears

7- What candy bar is made with chocolate, caramel, and peanuts?
A) Snickers B) Kit Kat

8- What candy is known for having a hard candy shell with a soft, chewy center?
A) Skittles B) Starburst

9- What candy is shaped like a small pellet and has a sour taste?
A) Warheads B) Hot Tamales

10- What candy is made with a chocolate shell and a creamy filling?
A) Lindt Truffles B) Reese's Peanut Butter Cups

11- What candy is a combination of chocolate and peanut butter?
A) Reese's Peanut Butter Cups B) 3 Musketeers

12- What candy is shaped like a small tube and has a fruit-flavored filling?
A) Twizzlers B) Sour Punch Straws

13- What candy is known for being a "minty fresh" breath freshener?
A) Altoids B) Lifesavers

14- What candy is a combination of chocolate, caramel, and cookie pieces?
A) Twix B) Kit Kat

15- What candy is shaped like a small cylinder and has a fruity flavor?
A) Nerds B) Mike and Ike

16- What candy bar is made with chocolate, caramel, and nougat, and is shaped like a long, thin rectangle?
A) Milky Way B) 3 Musketeers

17- What candy is shaped like a small bean and has a fruit-flavored shell with a jelly center?
A) Jelly Belly B) Skittles

18- What candy is shaped like a small disk and has a hard candy shell with a minty center?
A) Mentos B) Life Savers

19- What candy bar is made with chocolate, caramel, and wafer layers?
A) Kit Kat B) Twix

20- What candy is shaped like a small cone and is filled with ice cream?
A) Drumstick B) Snickers Ice Cream Bar

ANSWERS

1- What candy bar is made with nougat, caramel, and peanuts?
A) Snickers B) Butterfinger
Answer: A) Snickers

2- What candy is shaped like a bottle and has a cola flavor?
A) Cola Bottles B) Gummy Bears
Answer: A) Cola Bottles

3- What candy brand makes "Fun Dip"?
A) Wonka B) Reese's
Answer: A) Wonka

4- What candy is shaped like a small ball and has a hard outer shell with a chewy center?
A) Jawbreakers B) M&Ms
Answer: A) Jawbreakers

5- What candy is a combination of chocolate, caramel, and nougat?
A) Milky Way B) Twix
Answer: A) Milky Way

6- What candy is shaped like a small fish and has a fruity flavor?
A) Swedish Fish B) Gummi Bears
Answer: A) Swedish Fish

7- What candy bar is made with chocolate, caramel, and peanuts?
A) Snickers B) Kit Kat
Answer: A) Snickers

8- What candy is known for having a hard candy shell with a soft, chewy center?
A) Skittles B) Starburst
Answer: B) Starburst

9- What candy is shaped like a small pellet and has a sour taste?
A) Warheads B) Hot Tamales
Answer: A) Warheads

10- What candy is made with a chocolate shell and a creamy filling?
A) Lindt Truffles B) Reese's Peanut Butter Cups
Answer: A) Lindt Truffles

11- What candy is a combination of chocolate and peanut butter?
A) Reese's Peanut Butter Cups B) 3 Musketeers
Answer: A) Reese's Peanut Butter Cups

12- What candy is shaped like a small tube and has a fruit-flavored filling?
A) Twizzlers B) Sour Punch Straws
Answer: A) Twizzlers

13- What candy is known for being a "minty fresh" breath freshener?
A) Altoids B) Lifesavers
Answer: A) Altoids

14- What candy is a combination of chocolate, caramel, and cookie pieces?
A) Twix B) Kit Kat
Answer: A) Twix

15- What candy is shaped like a small cylinder and has a fruity flavor?
A) Nerds B) Mike and Ike
Answer: B) Mike and Ike

16- What candy bar is made with chocolate, caramel, and nougat, and is shaped like a long, thin rectangle?
A) Milky Way B) 3 Musketeers
Answer: B) 3 Musketeers

17- What candy is shaped like a small bean and has a fruit-flavored shell with a jelly center?
A) Jelly Belly B) Skittles
Answer: A) Jelly Belly

18- What candy is shaped like a small disk and has a hard candy shell with a minty center?
A) Mentos B) Life Savers
Answer: B) Life Savers

19- What candy bar is made with chocolate, caramel, and wafer layers?
A) Kit Kat B) Twix
Answer: B) Twix

20- What candy is shaped like a small cone and is filled with ice cream?
A) Drumstick B) Snickers Ice Cream Bar
Answer: A) Drumstick

1- What is the name of the cheese that is made from goat's milk?
A) Chevre
B) Roquefort

2- What is the name of the cheese that is made from sheep's milk?
A) Parmesan
B) Pecorino

3- What is the name of the cheese that is made from cow's milk and is often used on pizza?
A) Gouda
B) Mozzarella

4- What is the name of the cheese that is made from cow's milk and has holes in it?
A) Swiss
B) Cheddar

5- What is the name of the cheese that is made from buffalo's milk and is often used in Italian cuisine?
A) Brie
B) Buffalo mozzarella

6- What is the name of the cheese that is made from sheep's milk and is often used in Greek cuisine?
A) Feta
B) Camembert

7- What is the name of the cheese that is made from goat's milk and is often used in French cuisine?
A) Cheddar
B) Chevre

8- What is the name of the cheese that is made from cow's milk and is often used in Mexican cuisine?
A) Cheddar
B) Queso fresco

9- What is the name of the cheese that is made from sheep's milk and is often used in Spanish cuisine?
A) Gouda
B) Manchego

10- What is the name of the cheese that is made from cow's milk and is often used in English cuisine?
A) Brie
B) Cheddar

11- What is the name of the cheese that is made from goat's milk and is often used in Moroccan cuisine?
A) Halloumi
B) Chèvre

12- What is the name of the cheese that is made from sheep's milk and is often used in Italian cuisine?
A) Pecorino
B) Gouda

13- What is the name of the cheese that is made from cow's milk and is often used in French cuisine?
A) Camembert
B) Monterey Jack

14- What is the name of the cheese that is made from sheep's milk and is often used in Turkish cuisine?
A) Gouda
B) Feta

15- What is the name of the cheese that is made from cow's milk and is often used in Swiss cuisine?
A) Raclette
B) Havarti

16- What is the name of the cheese that is made from goat's milk and is often used in Spanish cuisine?
A) Cheddar
B) Cabrales

17- What is the name of the cheese that is made from cow's milk and is often used in American cuisine?
A) Monterey Jack
B) Brie

18- What is the name of the cheese that is made from sheep's milk and is often used in Greek cuisine?
A) Halloumi
B) Kefalotyri

19- What is the name of the cheese that is made from cow's milk and is often used in German cuisine?
A) Camembert
B) Butterkäse

20- What is the name of the cheese that is made from goat's milk and is often used in Italian cuisine?
A) Ricotta
B) Caprino

21- What is the name of the cheese that is made from cow's milk and is often used in Dutch cuisine?
A) Edam
B) Blue cheese

ANSWERS

1- What is the name of the cheese that is made from goat's milk?
A) Chevre (Answer)
B) Roquefort

2- What is the name of the cheese that is made from sheep's milk?
A) Parmesan
B) Pecorino (Answer)

3- What is the name of the cheese that is made from cow's milk and is often used on pizza?
A) Gouda
B) Mozzarella (Answer)

4- What is the name of the cheese that is made from cow's milk and has holes in it?
A) Swiss (Answer)
B) Cheddar

5- What is the name of the cheese that is made from buffalo's milk and is often used in Italian cuisine?
A) Brie
B) Buffalo mozzarella (Answer)

6- What is the name of the cheese that is made from sheep's milk and is often used in Greek cuisine?
A) Feta (Answer)
B) Camembert

7- What is the name of the cheese that is made from goat's milk and is often used in French cuisine?
A) Cheddar
B) Chevre (Answer)

8- What is the name of the cheese that is made from cow's milk and is often used in Mexican cuisine?
A) Cheddar
B) Queso fresco (Answer)

9- What is the name of the cheese that is made from sheep's milk and is often used in Spanish cuisine?
A) Gouda
B) Manchego (Answer)

10- What is the name of the cheese that is made from cow's milk and is often used in English cuisine?
A) Brie
B) Cheddar (Answer)

11- What is the name of the cheese that is made from goat's milk and is often used in Moroccan cuisine?
A) Halloumi
B) Chèvre (Answer)

12- What is the name of the cheese that is made from sheep's milk and is often used in Italian cuisine?
A) Pecorino (Answer)
B) Gouda

13- What is the name of the cheese that is made from cow's milk and is often used in French cuisine?
A) Camembert (Answer)
B) Monterey Jack

14- What is the name of the cheese that is made from sheep's milk and is often used in Turkish cuisine?
A) Gouda
B) Feta (Answer)

15- What is the name of the cheese that is made from cow's milk and is often used in Swiss cuisine?
A) Raclette (Answer)
B) Havarti

16- What is the name of the cheese that is made from goat's milk and is often used in Spanish cuisine?
A) Cheddar
B) Cabrales (Answer)

17- What is the name of the cheese that is made from cow's milk and is often used in American cuisine?
A) Monterey Jack (Answer)
B) Brie

18- What is the name of the cheese that is made from sheep's milk and is often used in Greek cuisine?
A) Halloumi
B) Kefalotyri (Answer)

19- What is the name of the cheese that is made from cow's milk and is often used in German cuisine?
A) Camembert
B) Butterkäse (Answer)

20- What is the name of the cheese that is made from goat's milk and is often used in Italian cuisine?
A) Ricotta
B) Caprino (Answer)

21- What is the name of the cheese that is made from cow's milk and is often used in Dutch cuisine?
A) Edam (Answer)
B) Blue cheese

1. What is the name of the fish that is often considered a symbol of good luck?
A) Koi
B) Piranha

2. What is the name of the fish that can live in both saltwater and freshwater?
A) Salmon
B) Anglerfish

3. What is the name of the fish that is known for its bright orange flesh?
A) Trout
B) Haddock

4. What is the name of the fish that is known for its long, narrow body and sharp teeth?
A) Barracuda
B) Goldfish

5. What is the name of the fish that is commonly used in sushi?
A) Tuna
B) Catfish

6. What is the name of the fish that is capable of shooting water out of its mouth to catch prey?
A) Archerfish
B) Clownfish

7. What is the name of the fish that is known for its ability to produce pearls?
A) Oyster
B) Trout

What is the name of the fish that is considered a delicacy in many parts of the world?
A) Caviar
B) Sardine

What is the name of the fish that is known for its circular shape and lack of a tail fin?
A) Sunfish
B) Swordfish

What is the name of the fish that is known for its ability to swim against strong currents?
A) Salmon
B) Carp

What is the name of the fish that is known for its ability to change its gender?
A) Clownfish
B) Tuna

What is the name of the fish that is known for its ability to survive in extreme temperatures?
A) Icefish
B) Goldfish

What is the name of the fish that is known for its long, sharp bill?
A) Swordfish
B) Trout

What is the name of the fish that is known for its ability to stick to surfaces using its modified fins?
A) Remora
B) Salmon

What is the name of the fish that is known for its bright, vibrant colors?
A) Angelfish
B) Catfish

What is the name of the fish that is commonly used to make fish and chips?
A) Cod
B) Tilapia

What is the name of the fish that is known for its electric shock ability?
A) Electric Eel
B) Clownfish

What is the name of the fish that is considered to be the fastest-swimming fish in the ocean?
A) Sailfish
B) Flounder

What is the name of the fish that is known for its ability to hide in plain sight by changing its color?
A) Octopus
B) Cuttlefish

What is the name of the fish that is commonly used in fish tacos?
A) Mahi Mahi
B) Haddock

ANSWERS

1. What is the name of the fish that is often considered a symbol of good luck?
A) Koi
B) Piranha
Answer: A) Koi

2. What is the name of the fish that can live in both saltwater and freshwater?
A) Salmon
B) Anglerfish
Answer: A) Salmon

3. What is the name of the fish that is known for its bright orange flesh?
A) Trout
B) Haddock
Answer: A) Trout

4. What is the name of the fish that is known for its long, narrow body and sharp teeth?
A) Barracuda
B) Goldfish
Answer: A) Barracuda

5. What is the name of the fish that is commonly used in sushi?
A) Tuna
B) Catfish
Answer: A) Tuna

6. What is the name of the fish that is capable of shooting water out of its mouth to catch prey?
A) Archerfish
B) Clownfish
Answer: A) Archerfish

7. What is the name of the fish that is known for its ability to produce pearls?
A) Oyster
B) Trout
Answer: A) Oyster

What is the name of the fish that is considered a delicacy in many parts of the world?
A) Caviar
B) Sardine
Answer: A) Caviar

What is the name of the fish that is known for its circular shape and lack of a tail fin?
A) Sunfish
B) Swordfish
Answer: A) Sunfish

What is the name of the fish that is known for its ability to swim against strong currents?
A) Salmon
B) Carp
Answer: A) Salmon

What is the name of the fish that is known for its ability to change its gender?
A) Clownfish
B) Tuna
Answer: A) Clownfish

What is the name of the fish that is known for its ability to survive in extreme temperatures?
A) Icefish
B) Goldfish
Answer: A) Icefish

What is the name of the fish that is known for its long, sharp bill?
A) Swordfish
B) Trout
Answer: A) Swordfish

What is the name of the fish that is known for its ability to stick to surfaces using its modified fins?
A) Remora
B) Salmon
Answer: A) Remora

What is the name of the fish that is known for its bright, vibrant colors?
A) Angelfish
B) Catfish
Answer: A) Angelfish

What is the name of the fish that is commonly used to make fish and chips?
A) Cod
B) Tilapia
Answer: A) Cod

What is the name of the fish that is known for its electric shock ability?
A) Electric Eel
B) Clownfish
Answer: A) Electric Eel

What is the name of the fish that is considered to be the fastest-swimming fish in the ocean?
A) Sailfish
B) Flounder
Answer: A) Sailfish

What is the name of the fish that is known for its ability to hide in plain sight by changing its color?
A) Octopus
B) Cuttlefish
Answer: B) Cuttlefish

What is the name of the fish that is commonly used in fish tacos?
A) Mahi Mahi
B) Haddock
Answer: A) Mahi Mahi

1- What is the largest city in China?
A) Shanghai
B) Beijing

2- What is the official language of China?
A) Mandarin
B) Cantonese

3- What is the name of the river that is considered the "mother river" of China?
A) Yellow River
B) Yangtze River

4- What is the name of the largest dam in China?
A) Three Gorges Dam
B) Hoover Dam

5- What is the name of the mountain range that is considered the "spine of China"?
A) Himalayas
B) Kunlun Mountains

6- What is the name of the ancient trade route that connected China to the Mediterranean world?
A) Silk Road
B) Spice Route

7- What is the name of the famous temple complex in Beijing that is known for its intricate architecture?
A) Forbidden City
B) Temple of Heaven

8- What is the name of the Chinese philosophy that emphasizes the importance of harmony and balance in all aspects of life?
A) Confucianism
B) Taoism

9- What is the name of the largest province in China by area?
A) Xinjiang
B) Sichuan

10- What is the name of the traditional Chinese martial art that is practiced for both self-defense and health benefits?
A) Tai Chi
B) Kung Fu

11- What is the name of the famous terracotta army that was discovered in China in 1974?
A) Qin Shi Huang's Army
B) Han Dynasty Warriors

12- What is the name of the Chinese holiday that celebrates the lunar new year?
A) Dragon Boat Festival
B) Spring Festival

13- What is the name of the city in China that is known for its spicy cuisine?
A) Chengdu
B) Hangzhou

14- What is the name of the Chinese invention that revolutionized printing in the world?
A) Gunpowder
B) Moveable Type Printing

15- What is the name of the Chinese philosopher who is known for his teachings on ethics and social relationships?
A) Confucius
B) Laozi

16- What is the name of the world's largest public square located in the heart of Beijing?
A) Tiananmen Square
B) People's Square

17- What is the name of the famous Chinese dynasty that was known for its art, culture, and poetry?
A) Tang Dynasty
B) Han Dynasty

18- What is the name of the Chinese dish that is made with thin noodles and a variety of toppings?
A) Dumplings
B) Chow Mein

19- What is the name of the Chinese holiday that celebrates the life and accomplishments of ancestors?
A) Qingming Festival
B) Mid-Autumn Festival

ANSWERS

1- What is the largest city in China?
A) Shanghai
B) Beijing
Right Answer: A) Shanghai

2- What is the official language of China?
A) Mandarin
B) Cantonese
Right Answer: A) Mandarin

3- What is the name of the river that is considered the "mother river" of China?
A) Yellow River
B) Yangtze River
Right Answer: A) Yellow River

4- What is the name of the largest dam in China?
A) Three Gorges Dam
B) Hoover Dam
Right Answer: A) Three Gorges Dam

5- What is the name of the mountain range that is considered the "spine of China"?
A) Himalayas
B) Kunlun Mountains
Right Answer: B) Kunlun Mountains

6- What is the name of the ancient trade route that connected China to the Mediterranean world?
A) Silk Road
B) Spice Route
Right Answer: A) Silk Road

7- What is the name of the famous temple complex in Beijing that is known for its intricate architecture?
A) Forbidden City
B) Temple of Heaven
Right Answer: B) Temple of Heaven

8- What is the name of the Chinese philosophy that emphasizes the importance of harmony and balance in all aspects of life?
A) Confucianism
B) Taoism
Right Answer: B) Taoism

9- What is the name of the largest province in China by area?
A) Xinjiang
B) Sichuan
Right Answer: A) Xinjiang

10- What is the name of the traditional Chinese martial art that is practiced for both self-defense and health benefits?
A) Tai Chi
B) Kung Fu
Right Answer: A) Tai Chi

11- What is the name of the famous terracotta army that was discovered in China in 1974?
A) Qin Shi Huang's Army
B) Han Dynasty Warriors
Right Answer: A) Qin Shi Huang's Army

12- What is the name of the Chinese holiday that celebrates the lunar new year?
A) Dragon Boat Festival
B) Spring Festival
Right Answer: B) Spring Festival

13- What is the name of the city in China that is known for its spicy cuisine?
A) Chengdu
B) Hangzhou
Right Answer: A) Chengdu

14- What is the name of the Chinese invention that revolutionized printing in the world?
A) Gunpowder
B) Moveable Type Printing
Right Answer: B) Moveable Type Printing

15- What is the name of the Chinese philosopher who is known for his teachings on ethics and social relationships?
A) Confucius
B) Laozi
Right Answer: A) Confucius

16- What is the name of the world's largest public square located in the heart of Beijing?
A) Tiananmen Square
B) People's Square
Right Answer: A) Tiananmen Square

17- What is the name of the famous Chinese dynasty that was known for its art, culture, and poetry?
A) Tang Dynasty
B) Han Dynasty
Right Answer: A) Tang Dynasty

18- What is the name of the Chinese dish that is made with thin noodles and a variety of toppings?
A) Dumplings
B) Chow Mein
Right Answer: B) Chow Mein

19- What is the name of the Chinese holiday that celebrates the life and accomplishments of ancestors?
A) Qingming Festival
B) Mid-Autumn Festival
Right Answer: A) Qingming Festival

1. What is the name of the animal that is known for producing wool?
A) Sheep
B) Goat

2. What is the name of the animal that produces milk for human consumption?
A) Cow
B) Horse

3. What is the name of the animal that is used for transportation and farming?
A) Donkey
B) Horse

4. What is the name of the animal that is often used to hunt rodents?
A) Cat
B) Barn owl

5. What is the name of the animal that is known for laying eggs?
A) Duck
B) Turkey

6. What is the name of the animal that is known for its curly tail?
A) Pig
B) Cow

7. What is the name of the animal that is known for its ability to provide eggs, meat, and feathers?
A) Chicken
B) Duck

8. What is the name of the animal that is known for its soft fur and is often kept as a pet?
A) Rabbit
B) Guinea pig

9. What is the name of the animal that is often used for meat and leather production?
A) Sheep
B) Cow

10. What is the name of the animal that is known for its large, curved horns?
A) Bull
B) Ram

11. What is the name of the animal that is often used for plowing fields and transportation in developing countries?
A) Elephant
B) Water buffalo

12. What is the name of the animal that is often used for dairy production in India?
A) Cow
B) Water buffalo

13. What is the name of the animal that is known for its ability to climb trees and produce milk?
A) Goat
B) Capybara

14. What is the name of the animal that is known for its ability to produce milk with a high butterfat content?
A) Goat
B) Jersey cow

15. What is the name of the animal that is known for its ability to provide meat, milk, and wool?
A) Llama
B) Alpaca

16. What is the name of the animal that is often used for its meat and hides?
A) Pig
B) Deer

17. What is the name of the animal that is known for its long neck and ability to reach high branches for food?
A) Giraffe
B) Horse

18. What is the name of the animal that is known for its ability to provide milk for human consumption and is often used for transportation in the Middle East?
A) Camel
B) Horse

19. What is the name of the animal that is often used for its meat and hides in the Western United States?
A) Cow
B) Bison

20. What is the name of the animal that is often used for its wool and is known for its gentle nature?
A) Sheep
B) Alpaca

21. What is the name of the animal that is often used for its meat and is known for its curly coat?
A) Sheep
B) Pig

22. What is the name of the animal that is often used for its milk and is known for its gentle, docile nature?
A) Cow
B) Goat

23. What is the name of the animal that is known for its large, floppy ears and is often used for meat production?
A) Cow
B) Rabbit

ANSWERS

1. What is the name of the animal that is known for producing wool?
A) Sheep (Answer)
B) Goat

2. What is the name of the animal that produces milk for human consumption?
A) Cow (Answer)
B) Horse

3. What is the name of the animal that is used for transportation and farming?
A) Donkey
B) Horse (Answer)

4. What is the name of the animal that is often used to hunt rodents?
A) Cat
B) Barn owl (Answer)

5. What is the name of the animal that is known for laying eggs?
A) Duck (Answer)
B) Turkey

6. What is the name of the animal that is known for its curly tail?
A) Pig (Answer)
B) Cow

7. What is the name of the animal that is known for its ability to provide eggs, meat, and feathers?
A) Chicken (Answer)
B) Duck

8. What is the name of the animal that is known for its soft fur and is often kept as a pet?
A) Rabbit (Answer)
B) Guinea pig

9. What is the name of the animal that is often used for meat and leather production?
A) Sheep
B) Cow (Answer)

10. What is the name of the animal that is known for its large, curved horns?
A) Bull (Answer)
B) Ram

11. What is the name of the animal that is often used for plowing fields and transportation in developing countries?
A) Elephant
B) Water buffalo (Answer)

12. What is the name of the animal that is often used for dairy production in India?
A) Cow
B) Water buffalo (Answer)

13. What is the name of the animal that is known for its ability to climb trees and produce milk?
A) Goat
B) Capybara (Answer)

14. What is the name of the animal that is known for its ability to produce milk with a high butterfat content?
A) Goat
B) Jersey cow (Answer)

15. What is the name of the animal that is known for its ability to provide meat, milk, and wool?
A) Llama (Answer)
B) Alpaca

16. What is the name of the animal that is often used for its meat and hides?
A) Pig
B) Deer (Answer)

17. What is the name of the animal that is known for its long neck and ability to reach high branches for food?
A) Giraffe
B) Horse (Answer)

18. What is the name of the animal that is known for its ability to provide milk for human consumption and is often used for transportation in the Middle East?
A) Camel (Answer)
B) Horse

19. What is the name of the animal that is often used for its meat and hides in the Western United States?
A) Cow
B) Bison (Answer)

20. What is the name of the animal that is often used for its wool and is known for its gentle nature?
A) Sheep (Answer)
B) Alpaca

21. What is the name of the animal that is often used for its meat and is known for its curly coat?
A) Sheep
B) Pig (Answer)

22. What is the name of the animal that is often used for its milk and is known for its gentle, docile nature?
A) Cow (Answer)
B) Goat

23. What is the name of the animal that is known for its large, floppy ears and is often used for meat production?
A) Cow
B) Rabbit (Answer)

1- What is the name of the dish made with long, thin noodles, tomato sauce, and meatballs?
A) Spaghetti and meatballs
B) Fettuccine Alfredo

2- What is the name of the cheese that is often grated on pasta dishes?
A) Parmesan
B) Cheddar

3- What is the name of the Italian cured meat that is often served with cheese and olives?
A) Prosciutto
B) Pepperoni

4- What is the name of the Italian bread that is traditionally made with olive oil and rosemary?
A) Focaccia
B) Baguette

5- What is the name of the Italian soup that is made with vegetables and beans?
A) Minestrone
B) Tomato soup

6- What is the name of the Italian dish that is made with rice, saffron, and various meats or seafood?
A) Risotto
B) Paella

7- What is the name of the Italian dish that is made with layers of pasta, cheese, and meat sauce?
A) Lasagna
B) Spaghetti carbonara

8- What is the name of the Italian dessert that is made with layers of sponge cake, cream, and coffee?
A) Tiramisu
B) Cannoli

9- What is the name of the Italian cheese that is often used in pizza and pasta dishes?
A) Mozzarella
B) Blue cheese

10- What is the name of the Italian dish that is made with tomato sauce, cheese, and toppings on a flatbread crust?
A) Pizza
B) Calzone

11- What is the name of the Italian dish that is made with breaded and fried veal or chicken, and is often served with spaghetti?
A) Chicken or Veal Parmesan
B) Chicken or Veal Marsala

12- What is the name of the Italian dessert that is made with sweetened ricotta cheese and chocolate chips?
A) Cannoli
B) Chocolate chip cannoli filling

13- What is the name of the Italian dessert that is made with cream, sugar, and gelatin?
A) Panna cotta
B) Tiramisu

14- What is the name of the Italian dessert that is made with fried dough and powdered sugar?
A) Zeppole
B) Cannoli

15- What is the name of the Italian dish that is made with clams, garlic, and white wine?
A) Linguine with Clams
B) Fettuccine Alfredo

16- What is the name of the Italian dish that is made with eggplant, tomato sauce, and cheese?
A) Eggplant Parmesan
B) Eggplant Lasagna

17- What is the name of the Italian pasta that is shaped like a bowtie?
A) Farfalle
B) Spaghetti

18- What is the name of the Italian pasta that is shaped like a tube?
A) Penne
B) Linguine

19- What is the name of the Italian dish that is made with Arborio rice, saffron, and seafood?
A) Seafood Risotto
B) Paella

20- What is the name of the Italian dish that is made with clams, mussels, shrimp, and calamari, served over linguine in a tomato sauce?
A) Seafood Fra Diavolo
B) Shrimp Scampi

ANSWERS

1- What is the name of the dish made with long, thin noodles, tomato sauce, and meatballs?
A) Spaghetti and meatballs (Answer)
B) Fettuccine Alfredo

2- What is the name of the cheese that is often grated on pasta dishes?
A) Parmesan (Answer)
B) Cheddar

3- What is the name of the Italian cured meat that is often served with cheese and olives?
A) Prosciutto (Answer)
B) Pepperoni

4- What is the name of the Italian bread that is traditionally made with olive oil and rosemary?
A) Focaccia (Answer)
B) Baguette

5- What is the name of the Italian soup that is made with vegetables and beans?
A) Minestrone (Answer)
B) Tomato soup

6- What is the name of the Italian dish that is made with rice, saffron, and various meats or seafood?
A) Risotto (Answer)
B) Paella

7- What is the name of the Italian dish that is made with layers of pasta, cheese, and meat sauce?
A) Lasagna (Answer)
B) Spaghetti carbonara

8- What is the name of the Italian dessert that is made with layers of sponge cake, cream, and coffee?
A) Tiramisu (Answer)
B) Cannoli

9- What is the name of the Italian cheese that is often used in pizza and pasta dishes?
A) Mozzarella (Answer)
B) Blue cheese

10- What is the name of the Italian dish that is made with tomato sauce, cheese, and toppings on a flatbread crust?
A) Pizza (Answer)
B) Calzone

11- What is the name of the Italian dish that is made with breaded and fried veal or chicken, and is often served with spaghetti?
A) Chicken or Veal Parmesan (Answer)
B) Chicken or Veal Marsala

12- What is the name of the Italian dessert that is made with sweetened ricotta cheese and chocolate chips?
A) Cannoli
B) Chocolate chip cannoli filling (Answer)

13- What is the name of the Italian dessert that is made with cream, sugar, and gelatin?
A) Panna cotta (Answer)
B) Tiramisu

14- What is the name of the Italian dessert that is made with fried dough and powdered sugar?
A) Zeppole (Answer)
B) Cannoli

15- What is the name of the Italian dish that is made with clams, garlic, and white wine?
A) Linguine with Clams (Answer)
B) Fettuccine Alfredo

16- What is the name of the Italian dish that is made with eggplant, tomato sauce, and cheese?
A) Eggplant Parmesan (Answer)
B) Eggplant Lasagna

17- What is the name of the Italian pasta that is shaped like a bowtie?
A) Farfalle (Answer)
B) Spaghetti

18- What is the name of the Italian pasta that is shaped like a tube?
A) Penne (Answer)
B) Linguine

19- What is the name of the Italian dish that is made with Arborio rice, saffron, and seafood?
A) Seafood Risotto (Answer)
B) Paella

20- What is the name of the Italian dish that is made with clams, mussels, shrimp, and calamari, served over linguine in a tomato sauce?
A) Seafood Fra Diavolo (Answer)
B) Shrimp Scampi

1. What is the name of the popular ice cream flavor that features vanilla ice cream, chunks of cookie dough, and chocolate chips?
A) Cookie Dough
B) Cookies and Cream

2. What is the name of the popular ice cream flavor that features chocolate ice cream, marshmallows, and nuts?
A) Rocky Road
B) Chocolate Chip

3. What is the name of the popular ice cream flavor that features strawberry ice cream and pieces of real strawberries?
A) Strawberry
B) Raspberry

4. What is the name of the popular ice cream flavor that features vanilla ice cream and swirls of caramel?
A) Caramel Swirl
B) Butterscotch

5. What is the name of the popular ice cream flavor that features chocolate ice cream and swirls of peanut butter?
A) Peanut Butter Cup
B) Chocolate Fudge

6. What is the name of the popular ice cream flavor that features vanilla ice cream and chunks of candy bars?
A) Candy Bar Crunch
B) Butter Pecan

7. What is the name of the popular ice cream flavor that features chocolate ice cream and pieces of chocolate-covered toffee?
A) Heath Bar Crunch
B) Chocolate Almond

8. What is the name of the popular ice cream flavor that features vanilla ice cream and chunks of fresh banana?
A) Banana Cream Pie
B) Vanilla Bean

9. What is the name of the popular ice cream flavor that features chocolate ice cream, swirls of marshmallow, and pieces of graham cracker?
A) S'mores
B) Chocolate Marshmallow

10. What is the name of the popular ice cream flavor that features coffee ice cream and chunks of chocolate?
A) Mocha Chip
B) Coffee Toffee

11. What is the name of the popular ice cream flavor that features vanilla ice cream and pieces of pecans?
A) Butter Pecan
B) Maple Walnut

12. What is the name of the popular ice cream flavor that features chocolate ice cream and pieces of chocolate brownie?
A) Brownie Batter
B) Double Chocolate

13. What is the name of the popular ice cream flavor that features vanilla ice cream and swirls of strawberry sauce?
A) Strawberry Sundae
B) Vanilla Swirl

14. What is the name of the popular ice cream flavor that features chocolate ice cream and swirls of fudge?
A) Chocolate Fudge Brownie
B) Hot Fudge

15. What is the name of the popular ice cream flavor that features vanilla ice cream and swirls of caramel and chocolate?
A) Turtle Sundae
B) Salted Caramel

16. What is the name of the popular ice cream flavor that features mint ice cream and chunks of chocolate?
A) Mint Chocolate Chip
B) Peppermint Pattie

17. What is the name of the popular ice cream flavor that features vanilla ice cream and chunks of cookie?
A) Cookies and Cream
B) Cookie Dough

18. What is the name of the popular ice cream flavor that features chocolate ice cream and swirls of caramel and peanuts?
A) Snickers
B) Chocolate Caramel Crunch

19. What is the name of the popular ice cream flavor that features vanilla ice cream and swirls of raspberry sauce?
A) Raspberry Swirl
B) Strawberry Ripple

ANSWERS

1. What is the name of the popular ice cream flavor that features vanilla ice cream, chunks of cookie dough, and chocolate chips?
A) Cookie Dough (Answer)
B) Cookies and Cream

2. What is the name of the popular ice cream flavor that features chocolate ice cream, marshmallows, and nuts?
A) Rocky Road (Answer)
B) Chocolate Chip

3. What is the name of the popular ice cream flavor that features strawberry ice cream and pieces of real strawberries?
A) Strawberry (Answer)
B) Raspberry

4. What is the name of the popular ice cream flavor that features vanilla ice cream and swirls of caramel?
A) Caramel Swirl (Answer)
B) Butterscotch

5. What is the name of the popular ice cream flavor that features chocolate ice cream and swirls of peanut butter?
A) Peanut Butter Cup (Answer)
B) Chocolate Fudge

6. What is the name of the popular ice cream flavor that features vanilla ice cream and chunks of candy bars?
A) Candy Bar Crunch (Answer)
B) Butter Pecan

7. What is the name of the popular ice cream flavor that features chocolate ice cream and pieces of chocolate-covered toffee?
A) Heath Bar Crunch (Answer)
B) Chocolate Almond

8. What is the name of the popular ice cream flavor that features vanilla ice cream and chunks of fresh banana?
A) Banana Cream Pie (Answer)
B) Vanilla Bean

9. What is the name of the popular ice cream flavor that features chocolate ice cream, swirls of marshmallow, and pieces of graham cracker?
A) S'mores (Answer)
B) Chocolate Marshmallow

10. What is the name of the popular ice cream flavor that features coffee ice cream and chunks of chocolate?
A) Mocha Chip (Answer)
B) Coffee Toffee

11. What is the name of the popular ice cream flavor that features vanilla ice cream and pieces of pecans?
A) Butter Pecan (Answer)
B) Maple Walnut

12. What is the name of the popular ice cream flavor that features chocolate ice cream and pieces of chocolate brownie?
A) Brownie Batter (Answer)
B) Double Chocolate

13. What is the name of the popular ice cream flavor that features vanilla ice cream and swirls of strawberry sauce?
A) Strawberry Sundae (Answer)
B) Vanilla Swirl

14. What is the name of the popular ice cream flavor that features chocolate ice cream and swirls of fudge?
A) Chocolate Fudge Brownie (Answer)
B) Hot Fudge

15. What is the name of the popular ice cream flavor that features vanilla ice cream and swirls of caramel and chocolate?
A) Turtle Sundae (Answer)
B) Salted Caramel

16. What is the name of the popular ice cream flavor that features mint ice cream and chunks of chocolate?
A) Mint Chocolate Chip (Answer)
B) Peppermint Pattie

17. What is the name of the popular ice cream flavor that features vanilla ice cream and chunks of cookie?
A) Cookies and Cream (Answer)
B) Cookie Dough

18. What is the name of the popular ice cream flavor that features chocolate ice cream and swirls of caramel and peanuts?
A) Snickers (Answer)
B) Chocolate Caramel Crunch

19. What is the name of the popular ice cream flavor that features vanilla ice cream and swirls of raspberry sauce?
A) Raspberry Swirl (Answer)
B) Strawberry Ripple

1- What is the name of the famous mausoleum in Agra, India that was built in the 17th century?
A) Taj Mahal
B) Great Wall of China

2- What is the name of the ancient citadel located in Peru that was built by the Incas?
A) Machu Picchu
B) Colosseum

3- What is the name of the famous bell tower in Italy that leans at an angle?
A) Leaning Tower of Pisa
B) Eiffel Tower

4- What is the name of the famous monument in the United States that was built to honor the country's first president?
A) Washington Monument
B) Lincoln Memorial

5- What is the name of the ancient temple complex in Cambodia that was built in the 12th century?
A) Angkor Wat
B) Parthenon

6- What is the name of the famous palace located in France that was built during the 17th century?
A) Palace of Versailles
B) Buckingham Palace

7- What is the name of the famous clock tower located in London, England?
A) Big Ben
B) Tower Bridge

8- What is the name of the famous statue located in Rio de Janeiro, Brazil?
A) Christ the Redeemer
B) Statue of Liberty

9- What is the name of the famous suspension bridge located in San Francisco, California?
A) Golden Gate Bridge
B) Brooklyn Bridge

10- What is the name of the famous ancient arena located in Rome, Italy?
A) Colosseum
B) Machu Picchu

11- What is the name of the famous palace located in Spain that was built in the 14th century?
A) Alhambra
B) Buckingham Palace

12- What is the name of the famous cathedral located in Paris, France?
A) Notre Dame
B) St. Peter's Basilica

13- What is the name of the famous opera house located in Sydney, Australia?
A) Sydney Opera House
B) Royal Opera House

14- What is the name of the famous tower located in Dubai, United Arab Emirates?
A) Burj Khalifa
B) Eiffel Tower

15- What is the name of the famous castle located in Scotland that was built during the 13th century?
A) Edinburgh Castle
B) Neuschwanstein Castle

16- What is the name of the famous temple located in Japan that was built in the 7th century?
A) Horyu-ji Temple
B) Parthenon

17- What is the name of the famous fortress located in Israel that was built during the 14th century BC?
A) Masada
B) Tower of London

18- What is the name of the famous palace located in India that was built during the 18th century?
A) City Palace of Jaipur
B) Forbidden City

19- What is the name of the famous ruin located in Rome, Italy that was once a Roman temple?
A) Pantheon
B) Petra

20- What is the name of the famous skyscraper located in New York City, United States?
A) Empire State Building
B) Willis Tower

ANSWERS

1- What is the name of the famous mausoleum in Agra, India that was built in the 17th century?
A) Taj Mahal (Answer)
B) Great Wall of China

2- What is the name of the ancient citadel located in Peru that was built by the Incas?
A) Machu Picchu (Answer)
B) Colosseum

3- What is the name of the famous bell tower in Italy that leans at an angle?
A) Leaning Tower of Pisa (Answer)
B) Eiffel Tower

4- What is the name of the famous monument in the United States that was built to honor the country's first president?
A) Washington Monument (Answer)
B) Lincoln Memorial

5- What is the name of the ancient temple complex in Cambodia that was built in the 12th century?
A) Angkor Wat (Answer)
B) Parthenon

6- What is the name of the famous palace located in France that was built during the 17th century?
A) Palace of Versailles (Answer)
B) Buckingham Palace

7- What is the name of the famous clock tower located in London, England?
A) Big Ben (Answer)
B) Tower Bridge

8- What is the name of the famous statue located in Rio de Janeiro, Brazil?
A) Christ the Redeemer (Answer)
B) Statue of Liberty

9- What is the name of the famous suspension bridge located in San Francisco, California?
A) Golden Gate Bridge (Answer)
B) Brooklyn Bridge

10- What is the name of the famous ancient arena located in Rome, Italy?
A) Colosseum (Answer)
B) Machu Picchu

11- What is the name of the famous palace located in Spain that was built in the 14th century?
A) Alhambra (Answer)
B) Buckingham Palace

12- What is the name of the famous cathedral located in Paris, France?
A) Notre Dame (Answer)
B) St. Peter's Basilica

13- What is the name of the famous opera house located in Sydney, Australia?
A) Sydney Opera House (Answer)
B) Royal Opera House

14- What is the name of the famous tower located in Dubai, United Arab Emirates?
A) Burj Khalifa (Answer)
B) Eiffel Tower

15- What is the name of the famous castle located in Scotland that was built during the 13th century?
A) Edinburgh Castle (Answer)
B) Neuschwanstein Castle

16- What is the name of the famous temple located in Japan that was built in the 7th century?
A) Horyu-ji Temple (Answer)
B) Parthenon

17- What is the name of the famous fortress located in Israel that was built during the 14th century BC?
A) Masada (Answer)
B) Tower of London

18- What is the name of the famous palace located in India that was built during the 18th century?
A) City Palace of Jaipur (Answer)
B) Forbidden City

19- What is the name of the famous ruin located in Rome, Italy that was once a Roman temple?
A) Pantheon (Answer)
B) Petra

20- What is the name of the famous skyscraper located in New York City, United States?
A) Empire State Building (Answer)
B) Willis Tower

1- What is the capital city of Nevada?
A) Carson City
B) Las Vegas

2- Which famous man-made attraction is located on the Las Vegas Strip in Nevada?
A) The Bellagio Fountains
B) The Golden Gate Bridge

3- What is the name of the famous lake located on the border of California and Nevada?
A) Lake Tahoe
B) Lake Superior

4- Which national park is located in Nevada?
A) Great Basin National Park
B) Yellowstone National Park

5- What is the name of the famous highway that runs through Nevada and is known for its scenic views and historic landmarks?
A) Route 66
B) Highway 50, also known as the "Loneliest Road in America"

6- Which popular gambling destination is located in Nevada and is known as "The Biggest Little City in the World"?
A) Reno
B) Atlantic City

7- What is the name of the famous dam located on the Colorado River between Arizona and Nevada?
A) Hoover Dam
B) Grand Coulee Dam

8- Which famous festival that takes place annually in Nevada is known for its art installations, music performances, and unique culture?
A) Burning Man
B) Coachella

9- What is the name of the popular state park located in Nevada that is known for its red rock formations and hiking trails?
A) Valley of Fire State Park
B) Yellowstone National Park

10- Which city in Nevada is known as the "Entertainment Capital of the World"?
A) Las Vegas
B) Reno

11- What is the name of the famous street in Las Vegas that is known for its bright lights and large casinos?
A) The Strip
B) Broadway

12- Which famous hotel and casino in Las Vegas is known for its replica of the Eiffel Tower?
A) Paris Las Vegas
B) The Venetian

13- What is the name of the famous boxing venue located in Las Vegas that has hosted numerous championship fights?
A) MGM Grand Garden Arena
B) Madison Square Garden

14- What is the name of the famous ranch located in northern Nevada that was owned by the wealthy businessman Howard Hughes?
A) The Spruce Goose Ranch
B) The Flying M Ranch

15- Which famous celebrity was married in Las Vegas in 1967 and famously said, "What happens in Vegas, stays in Vegas"?
A) Elvis Presley
B) Frank Sinatra

16- Which college football bowl game takes place annually in Las Vegas?
A) Las Vegas Bowl
B) Orange Bowl

17- What is the name of the famous hotel and casino in Las Vegas that is shaped like a pyramid?
A) Luxor
B) Caesars Palace

18- Which famous singer had a long-running residency at Caesars Palace in Las Vegas?
A) Celine Dion
B) Britney Spears

19- What is the name of the popular theme park located in Las Vegas that features rides and attractions based on horror films?
A) Fright Dome
B) Six Flags Magic Mountain

20- Which famous author wrote a novel that was set in Las Vegas and later adapted into a movie starring Johnny Depp?
A) Hunter S. Thompson
B) Stephen King

ANSWERS

1- What is the capital city of Nevada?
A) Carson City (Answer)
B) Las Vegas

2- Which famous man-made attraction is located on the Las Vegas Strip in Nevada?
A) The Bellagio Fountains (Answer)
B) The Golden Gate Bridge

3- What is the name of the famous lake located on the border of California and Nevada?
A) Lake Tahoe (Answer)
B) Lake Superior

4- Which national park is located in Nevada?
A) Great Basin National Park (Answer)
B) Yellowstone National Park

5- What is the name of the famous highway that runs through Nevada and is known for its scenic views and historic landmarks?
A) Route 66
B) Highway 50, also known as the "Loneliest Road in America" (Answer)

6- Which popular gambling destination is located in Nevada and is known as "The Biggest Little City in the World"?
A) Reno (Answer)
B) Atlantic City

7- What is the name of the famous dam located on the Colorado River between Arizona and Nevada?
A) Hoover Dam (Answer)
B) Grand Coulee Dam

8- Which famous festival that takes place annually in Nevada is known for its art installations, music performances, and unique culture?
A) Burning Man (Answer)
B) Coachella

9- What is the name of the popular state park located in Nevada that is known for its red rock formations and hiking trails?
A) Valley of Fire State Park (Answer)
B) Yellowstone National Park

10- Which city in Nevada is known as the "Entertainment Capital of the World"?
A) Las Vegas (Answer)
B) Reno

11- What is the name of the famous street in Las Vegas that is known for its bright lights and large casinos?
A) The Strip (Answer)
B) Broadway

12- Which famous hotel and casino in Las Vegas is known for its replica of the Eiffel Tower?
A) Paris Las Vegas (Answer)
B) The Venetian

13- What is the name of the famous boxing venue located in Las Vegas that has hosted numerous championship fights?
A) MGM Grand Garden Arena (Answer)
B) Madison Square Garden

14- What is the name of the famous ranch located in northern Nevada that was owned by the wealthy businessman Howard Hughes?
A) The Spruce Goose Ranch
B) The Flying M Ranch (Answer)

15- Which famous celebrity was married in Las Vegas in 1967 and famously said, "What happens in Vegas, stays in Vegas"?
A) Elvis Presley (Answer)
B) Frank Sinatra

16- Which college football bowl game takes place annually in Las Vegas?
A) Las Vegas Bowl (Answer)
B) Orange Bowl

17- What is the name of the famous hotel and casino in Las Vegas that is shaped like a pyramid?
A) Luxor (Answer)
B) Caesars Palace

18- Which famous singer had a long-running residency at Caesars Palace in Las Vegas?
A) Celine Dion (Answer)
B) Britney Spears

19- What is the name of the popular theme park located in Las Vegas that features rides and attractions based on horror films?
A) Fright Dome (Answer)
B) Six Flags Magic Mountain

20- Which famous author wrote a novel that was set in Las Vegas and later adapted into a movie starring Johnny Depp?
A) Hunter S. Thompson (Answer)
B) Stephen King

1- Who is the author of "The Cat in the Hat"?
A) Dr. Seuss
B) J.K. Rowling

2- What is the title of the first book in the "Harry Potter" series?
A) The Philosopher's Stone
B) The Chamber of Secrets

3- Who wrote the children's book "Charlie and the Chocolate Factory"?
A) Roald Dahl
B) C.S. Lewis

4- What is the title of the book by Eric Carle about a caterpillar who eats his way through a variety of foods?
A) The Hungry Caterpillar
B) The Very Busy Spider

5- Who is the author of "Green Eggs and Ham"?
A) Dr. Seuss
B) Maurice Sendak

6- What is the title of the book by J.M. Barrie about a boy who never grows up?
A) Peter Pan
B) Alice in Wonderland

7- Who wrote "Where the Wild Things Are"?
A) Maurice Sendak
B) Eric Carle

8- What is the title of the book by E.B. White about a spider who befriends a pig?
A) Charlotte's Web
B) Stuart Little

9- Who is the author of "The Giving Tree"?
A) Shel Silverstein
B) Dr. Seuss

10- What is the title of the book by Lewis Carroll about a girl who falls down a rabbit hole?
A) Alice in Wonderland
B) The Secret Garden

11- Who wrote "The Polar Express"?
A) Chris Van Allsburg
B) Mo Willems

12- What is the title of the book by Margaret Wise Brown about a bunny saying goodnight to various objects in his room?
A) Goodnight Moon
B) The Very Hungry Caterpillar

13- Who is the author of "Corduroy"?
A) Don Freeman
B) Maurice Sendak

14- What is the title of the book by Norton Juster about a boy who explores a fantastical world?
A) The Phantom Tollbooth
B) A Wrinkle in Time

15- Who wrote "The Very Hungry Caterpillar"?
A) Eric Carle
B) Roald Dahl

16- What is the title of the book by Kenneth Grahame about a group of animal friends who live along a riverbank?
A) The Wind in the Willows
B) Charlotte's Web

17- Who wrote "James and the Giant Peach"?
A) Roald Dahl
B) J.K. Rowling

18- What is the title of the book by Lois Lowry about a young boy in a utopian society?
A) The Giver
B) The Catcher in the Rye

ANSWERS

1- Who is the author of "The Cat in the Hat"?
A) Dr. Seuss
B) J.K. Rowling
Answer: A) Dr. Seuss

2- What is the title of the first book in the "Harry Potter" series?
A) The Philosopher's Stone
B) The Chamber of Secrets
Answer: A) The Philosopher's Stone

3- Who wrote the children's book "Charlie and the Chocolate Factory"?
A) Roald Dahl
B) C.S. Lewis
Answer: A) Roald Dahl

4- What is the title of the book by Eric Carle about a caterpillar who eats his way through a variety of foods?
A) The Hungry Caterpillar
B) The Very Busy Spider
Answer: A) The Hungry Caterpillar

5- Who is the author of "Green Eggs and Ham"?
A) Dr. Seuss
B) Maurice Sendak
Answer: A) Dr. Seuss

6- What is the title of the book by J.M. Barrie about a boy who never grows up?
A) Peter Pan
B) Alice in Wonderland
Answer: A) Peter Pan

7- Who wrote "Where the Wild Things Are"?
A) Maurice Sendak
B) Eric Carle
Answer: A) Maurice Sendak

8- What is the title of the book by E.B. White about a spider who befriends a pig?
A) Charlotte's Web
B) Stuart Little
Answer: A) Charlotte's Web

9- Who is the author of "The Giving Tree"?
A) Shel Silverstein
B) Dr. Seuss
Answer: A) Shel Silverstein

10- What is the title of the book by Lewis Carroll about a girl who falls down a rabbit hole?
A) Alice in Wonderland
B) The Secret Garden
Answer: A) Alice in Wonderland

11- Who wrote "The Polar Express"?
A) Chris Van Allsburg
B) Mo Willems
Answer: A) Chris Van Allsburg

12- What is the title of the book by Margaret Wise Brown about a bunny saying goodnight to various objects in his room?
A) Goodnight Moon
B) The Very Hungry Caterpillar
Answer: A) Goodnight Moon

13- Who is the author of "Corduroy"?
A) Don Freeman
B) Maurice Sendak
Answer: A) Don Freeman

14- What is the title of the book by Norton Juster about a boy who explores a fantastical world?
A) The Phantom Tollbooth
B) A Wrinkle in Time
Answer: A) The Phantom Tollbooth

15- Who wrote "The Very Hungry Caterpillar"?
A) Eric Carle
B) Roald Dahl
Answer: A) Eric Carle

16- What is the title of the book by Kenneth Grahame about a group of animal friends who live along a riverbank?
A) The Wind in the Willows
B) Charlotte's Web
Answer: A) The Wind in the Willows

17- Who wrote "James and the Giant Peach"?
A) Roald Dahl
B) J.K. Rowling
Answer: A) Roald Dahl

18- What is the title of the book by Lois Lowry about a young boy in a utopian society?
A) The Giver
B) The Catcher in the Rye
Answer: A) The Giver

1- What is the deepest part of the ocean?
A) Challenger Deep
B) Marianas Trench

2- What is the largest ocean in the world?
A) Pacific Ocean
B) Indian Ocean

3- What is the name of the smallest ocean in the world?
A) Arctic Ocean
B) Southern Ocean

4- What is the name of the largest coral reef system in the world?
A) Great Barrier Reef
B) Red Sea Coral Reef

5- What is the name of the largest mammal in the world that lives in the ocean?
A) Dolphin
B) Blue Whale

6- What is the name of the marine animal that is often called the "sea cow" and is known for its gentle nature?
A) Walrus
B) Manatee

7- What is the process by which plants in the ocean produce energy using sunlight?
A) Photosynthesis
B) Respiration

8- What is the name of the phenomenon that occurs when the moon's gravitational pull affects the ocean's tides?
A) Lunar Cycle
B) Tide Cycle

9- What is the name of the ocean current that travels along the eastern coast of North America?
A) Gulf Stream
B) Pacific Current

10- What is the name of the bioluminescent marine animal that glows in the dark?
A) Jellyfish
B) Octopus

11- What is the name of the ocean that surrounds Antarctica?
A) Southern Ocean
B) Arctic Ocean

12- What is the name of the small, colorful fish that is often found in coral reefs?
A) Clownfish
B) Piranha

13- What is the name of the largest predator in the ocean?
A) Killer Whale
B) Great White Shark

14- What is the name of the phenomenon that occurs when warm water from an ocean current meets cold water from another current?
A) Oceanic Collision
B) Upwelling

15- What is the name of the process by which salt is removed from ocean water to make it drinkable?
A) Desalination
B) Distillation

16- What is the name of the underwater mountain range that runs through the Atlantic Ocean?
A) Mid-Atlantic Ridge
B) Pacific Ring of Fire

17- What is the name of the process by which marine animals shed their outer layer of skin?
A) Molting
B) Fossilization

18- What is the name of the ocean that is located between Asia and North America?
A) Pacific Ocean
B) Indian Ocean

19- What is the name of the marine animal that is known for its long tentacles and powerful sting?
A) Octopus
B) Jellyfish

20- What is the name of the ocean current that travels along the western coast of South America?
A) Humboldt Current
B) Atlantic Current

ANSWERS

1- What is the deepest part of the ocean?
A) Challenger Deep (Answer)
B) Marianas Trench

2- What is the largest ocean in the world?
A) Pacific Ocean (Answer)
B) Indian Ocean

3- What is the name of the smallest ocean in the world?
A) Arctic Ocean
B) Southern Ocean (Answer)

4- What is the name of the largest coral reef system in the world?
A) Great Barrier Reef (Answer)
B) Red Sea Coral Reef

5- What is the name of the largest mammal in the world that lives in the ocean?
A) Dolphin
B) Blue Whale (Answer)

6- What is the name of the marine animal that is often called the "sea cow" and is known for its gentle nature?
A) Walrus
B) Manatee (Answer)

7- What is the process by which plants in the ocean produce energy using sunlight?
A) Photosynthesis (Answer)
B) Respiration

8- What is the name of the phenomenon that occurs when the moon's gravitational pull affects the ocean's tides?
A) Lunar Cycle
B) Tide Cycle (Answer)

9- What is the name of the ocean current that travels along the eastern coast of North America?
A) Gulf Stream (Answer)
B) Pacific Current

10- What is the name of the bioluminescent marine animal that glows in the dark?
A) Jellyfish (Answer)
B) Octopus

11- What is the name of the ocean that surrounds Antarctica?
A) Southern Ocean (Answer)
B) Arctic Ocean

12- What is the name of the small, colorful fish that is often found in coral reefs?
A) Clownfish (Answer)
B) Piranha

13- What is the name of the largest predator in the ocean?
A) Killer Whale (Answer)
B) Great White Shark

14- What is the name of the phenomenon that occurs when warm water from an ocean current meets cold water from another current?
A) Oceanic Collision
B) Upwelling (Answer)

15- What is the name of the process by which salt is removed from ocean water to make it drinkable?
A) Desalination (Answer)
B) Distillation

16- What is the name of the underwater mountain range that runs through the Atlantic Ocean?
A) Mid-Atlantic Ridge (Answer)
B) Pacific Ring of Fire

17- What is the name of the process by which marine animals shed their outer layer of skin?
A) Molting (Answer)
B) Fossilization

18- What is the name of the ocean that is located between Asia and North America?
A) Pacific Ocean (Answer)
B) Indian Ocean

19- What is the name of the marine animal that is known for its long tentacles and powerful sting?
A) Octopus
B) Jellyfish (Answer)

20- What is the name of the ocean current that travels along the western coast of South America?
A) Humboldt Current (Answer)
B) Atlantic Current

1- What is the name of the sugar found in milk?
A) Lactose
B) Fructose

2- What is the name of the process used to make cheese from milk?
A) Fermentation
B) Coagulation

3- What is the name of the milk that is high in fat content?
A) Skim milk
B) Whole milk

4- What is the name of the milk that is low in fat content?
A) Whole milk
B) Skim milk

5- What is the name of the milk that is high in protein content?
A) Soy milk
B) Almond milk

6- What is the name of the milk that is lactose-free?
A) Soy milk
B) Lactaid milk

7- What is the name of the milk that is often used to make yogurt?
A) Goat milk
B) Cow milk

8- What is the name of the milk that is often used to make butter?
A) Goat milk
B) Cream

9- What is the name of the milk that is often used to make ice cream?
A) Heavy cream
B) Buttermilk

10- What is the name of the process used to extend the shelf life of milk?
A) Pasteurization
B) Fermentation

11- What is the name of the milk that is often used to make sour cream?
A) Heavy cream
B) Buttermilk

12- What is the name of the milk that is often used to make condensed milk?
A) Skim milk
B) Sweetened condensed milk

13- What is the name of the milk that is often used to make evaporated milk?
A) Whole milk
B) Evaporated milk

14- What is the name of the milk that is often used to make hot cocoa?
A) Soy milk
B) Whole milk

15- What is the name of the milk that is often used to make eggnog?
A) Heavy cream
B) Whole milk

16- What is the name of the milk that is often used to make cappuccino?
A) Skim milk
B) Foamed milk

17- What is the name of the milk that is often used to make latte?
A) Almond milk
B) Steamed milk

18- What is the name of the milk that is often used to make chai tea latte?
A) Coconut milk
B) Whole milk

19- What is the name of the milk that is often used to make milkshakes?
A) Almond milk
B) Vanilla ice cream

20- What is the name of the milk that is often used to make smoothies?
A) Skim milk
B) Greek yogurt

21- What is the name of the milk that is often used to make whipped cream?
A) Heavy cream
B) Buttermilk

22- What is the name of the milk that is often used to make eggnog latte?
A) Soy milk
B) Eggnog

23- What is the name of the milk that is often used to make café au lait?
A) Whole milk
B) Coconut milk

24- What is the name of the milk that is often used to make chocolate milk?
A) Skim milk
B) Whole milk

ANSWERS

1- What is the name of the sugar found in milk?
A) Lactose (Answer)
B) Fructose

2- What is the name of the process used to make cheese from milk?
A) Fermentation
B) Coagulation (Answer)

3- What is the name of the milk that is high in fat content?
A) Skim milk
B) Whole milk (Answer)

4- What is the name of the milk that is low in fat content?
A) Whole milk
B) Skim milk (Answer)

5- What is the name of the milk that is high in protein content?
A) Soy milk
B) Almond milk

6- What is the name of the milk that is lactose-free?
A) Soy milk
B) Lactaid milk (Answer)

7- What is the name of the milk that is often used to make yogurt?
A) Goat milk
B) Cow milk (Answer)

8- What is the name of the milk that is often used to make butter?
A) Goat milk B) Cream (Answer)

What is the name of the milk that is often used to make ice cream?
A) Heavy cream (Answer) B) Buttermilk

What is the name of the process used to extend the shelf life of milk?
A) Pasteurization (Answer)
B) Fermentation

What is the name of the milk that is often used to make sour cream?
A) Heavy cream
B) Buttermilk (Answer)

What is the name of the milk that is often used to make condensed milk?
A) Skim milk
B) Sweetened condensed milk (Answer)

What is the name of the milk that is often used to make evaporated milk?
A) Whole milk
B) Evaporated milk (Answer)

What is the name of the milk that is often used to make hot cocoa?
A) Soy milk
B) Whole milk (Answer)

What is the name of the milk that is often used to make eggnog?
A) Heavy cream
B) Whole milk (Answer)

What is the name of the milk that is often used to make cappuccino?
A) Skim milk
B) Foamed milk (Answer)

What is the name of the milk that is often used to make latte?
A) Almond milk
B) Steamed milk (Answer)

What is the name of the milk that is often used to make chai tea latte?
A) Coconut milk
B) Whole milk (Answer)

What is the name of the milk that is often used to make milkshakes?
A) Almond milk
B) Vanilla ice cream (Answer)

What is the name of the milk that is often used to make smoothies?
A) Skim milk
B) Greek yogurt (Answer)

What is the name of the milk that is often used to make whipped cream?
A) Heavy cream (Answer)
B) Buttermilk

What is the name of the milk that is often used to make eggnog latte?
A) Soy milk
B) Eggnog (Answer)

What is the name of the milk that is often used to make café au lait?
A) Whole milk (Answer)
B) Coconut milk

What is the name of the milk that is often used to make chocolate milk?
A) Skim milk
B) Whole milk (Answer)

1- What is the most common species of shark?
A) Great White Shark
B) Bull Shark

2- Do sharks have bones?
A) Yes
B) No

3- Can sharks smell blood from miles away?
A) Yes
B) No

4- Do sharks have eyelids?
A) Yes
B) No

5- Can sharks swim backwards?
A) Yes
B) No

6- What is the deadliest species of shark?
A) Tiger Shark
B) Hammerhead Shark

7- Do sharks lay eggs?
A) Yes
B) No

8- Can sharks jump out of the water?
A) Yes
B) No

9- Do sharks have a good sense of taste?
A) Yes
B) No

10- What is the most popular shark to eat?
A) Mako Shark
B) Lemon Shark

11- Can sharks hear well?
A) Yes
B) No

12- What is the lifespan of a shark?
A) 10-20 years
B) 70-100 years

13- Do sharks migrate?
A) Yes
B) No

14- Can sharks see colors?
A) Yes
B) No

15- What is the fastest species of shark?
A) Mako Shark
B) Nurse Shark

16- Are sharks warm-blooded?
A) Yes
B) No

17- Can sharks breathe through their mouths?
A) Yes
B) No

18- What is the most intelligent species of shark?
A) Great White Shark
B) Hammerhead Shark

19- Can sharks survive out of water for long periods of time?
A) Yes
B) No

20- Do sharks have a good memory?
A) Yes
B) No

21- What is the largest species of shark?
A) Tiger Shark
B) Whale Shark

22- Do sharks sleep?
A) Yes
B) No

23- What is the gestation period of a shark?
A) 3-4 months
B) 9-12 months

24- Can sharks regrow their teeth?
A) Yes
B) No

25- What is the smallest species of shark?
A) Blacktip Shark
B) Dwarf Lantern Shark

ANSWERS

1- What is the most common species of shark?
A) Great White Shark
B) Bull Shark (Answer)

2- Do sharks have bones?
A) Yes (Answer)
B) No

3- Can sharks smell blood from miles away?
A) Yes (Answer)
B) No

4- Do sharks have eyelids?
A) Yes
B) No (Answer)

5- Can sharks swim backwards?
A) Yes
B) No (Answer)

6- What is the deadliest species of shark?
A) Tiger Shark (Answer)
B) Hammerhead Shark

7- Do sharks lay eggs?
A) Yes
B) No (Answer)

8- Can sharks jump out of the water?
A) Yes (Answer)
B) No

9- Do sharks have a good sense of taste?
A) Yes (Answer)
B) No

10- What is the most popular shark to eat?
A) Mako Shark (Answer)
B) Lemon Shark

11- Can sharks hear well?
A) Yes (Answer)
B) No

12- What is the lifespan of a shark?
A) 10-20 years
B) 70-100 years (Answer)

13- Do sharks migrate?
A) Yes (Answer)
B) No

14- Can sharks see colors?
A) Yes
B) No (Answer)

15- What is the fastest species of shark?
A) Mako Shark (Answer)
B) Nurse Shark

16- Are sharks warm-blooded?
A) Yes
B) No (Answer)

17- Can sharks breathe through their mouths?
A) Yes
B) No (Answer)

18- What is the most intelligent species of shark?
A) Great White Shark
B) Hammerhead Shark (Answer)

19- Can sharks survive out of water for long periods of time?
A) Yes (Answer)
B) No

20- Do sharks have a good memory?
A) Yes (Answer)
B) No

21- What is the largest species of shark?
A) Tiger Shark
B) Whale Shark (Answer)

22- Do sharks sleep?
A) Yes (Answer)
B) No

23- What Is the gestation period of a shark?
A) 3-4 months
B) 9-12 months (Answer)

24- Can sharks regrow their teeth?
A) Yes (Answer)
B) No

25- What is the smallest species of shark?
A) Blacktip Shark
B) Dwarf Lantern Shark (Answer)

1- What is the name of the famous composer who wrote the opera The Magic Flute?
A) Wolfgang Amadeus Mozart
B) Ludwig van Beethoven

2- What is the name of the famous rock band that released the album The Wall?
A) Pink Floyd
B) The Beatles

3- What is the name of the famous American singer who is known as the Queen of Pop?
A) Madonna
B) Beyoncé

4- What is the name of the famous British singer who sang the song Rolling in the Deep?
A) Adele
B) Ed Sheeran

5- What is the name of the famous jazz trumpeter who was nicknamed Satchmo?
A) Louis Armstrong
B) Miles Davis

6- What is the name of the famous American rapper who released the album The Marshall Mathers LP?
A) Eminem
B) Jay-Z

7- What is the name of the famous British singer who sang the song Somebody That I Used to Know?
A) Gotye
B) Sam Smith

8- What is the name of the famous composer who wrote the ballet The Nutcracker?
A) Pyotr Ilyich Tchaikovsky
B) Johann Sebastian Bach

9- What is the name of the famous American singer who is known for her powerful voice and songs like I Will Always Love You?
A) Whitney Houston
B) Mariah Carey

10- What is the name of the famous British rock band that released the album Nevermind the Bollocks, Here's the Sex Pistols?
A) Sex Pistols
B) The Rolling Stones

11- What is the name of the famous American rapper who released the album All Eyez on Me?
A) Tupac Shakur
B) Notorious B.I.G.

12- What is the name of the famous Canadian singer who sang the song Sorry?
A) Justin Bieber
B) Drake

13- What is the name of the famous composer who wrote the opera La Traviata?
A) Giuseppe Verdi
B) Wolfgang Amadeus Mozart

14- What is the name of the famous American singer who is known for his smooth voice and songs like Fly Me to the Moon?
A) Frank Sinatra
B) Dean Martin

15- What is the name of the famous British band that released the album OK Computer?
A) Radiohead
B) Oasis

16- What is the name of the famous American singer who sang the song Toxic?
A) Britney Spears
B) Christina Aguilera

17- What is the name of the famous composer who wrote the opera Carmen?
A) Georges Bizet
B) Richard Wagner

18- What is the name of the famous American singer who is known for her unique voice and songs like Crazy?
A) Patsy Cline
B) Dolly Parton

19- What is the name of the famous British band that released the album Sgt. Pepper's Lonely Hearts Club Band?
A) The Beatles
B) The Rolling Stones

20- What is the name of the famous American singer who is known for her powerful voice and songs like Respect?
A) Aretha Franklin
B) Tina Turner

21- What is the name of the famous American band that released the album Nevermind?
A) Nirvana
B) Metallica

ANSWERS

1- What is the name of the famous composer who wrote the opera The Magic Flute?
A) Wolfgang Amadeus Mozart (Answer)
B) Ludwig van Beethoven

2- What is the name of the famous rock band that released the album The Wall?
A) Pink Floyd (Answer)
B) The Beatles

3- What is the name of the famous American singer who is known as the Queen of Pop?
A) Madonna (Answer)
B) Beyoncé

4- What is the name of the famous British singer who sang the song Rolling in the Deep?
A) Adele (Answer)
B) Ed Sheeran

5- What is the name of the famous jazz trumpeter who was nicknamed Satchmo?
A) Louis Armstrong (Answer)
B) Miles Davis

6- What is the name of the famous American rapper who released the album The Marshall Mathers LP?
A) Eminem (Answer)
B) Jay-Z

7- What is the name of the famous British singer who sang the song Somebody That I Used to Know?
A) Gotye (Answer)
B) Sam Smith

8- What is the name of the famous composer who wrote the ballet The Nutcracker?
A) Pyotr Ilyich Tchaikovsky (Answer)
B) Johann Sebastian Bach

9- What is the name of the famous American singer who is known for her powerful voice and songs like I Will Always Love You?
A) Whitney Houston (Answer)
B) Mariah Carey

10- What is the name of the famous British rock band that released the album Nevermind the Bollocks, Here's the Sex Pistols?
A) Sex Pistols (Answer)
B) The Rolling Stones

11- What is the name of the famous American rapper who released the album All Eyez on Me?
A) Tupac Shakur (Answer)
B) Notorious B.I.G.

12- What is the name of the famous Canadian singer who sang the song Sorry?
A) Justin Bieber (Answer)
B) Drake

13- What is the name of the famous composer who wrote the opera La Traviata?
A) Giuseppe Verdi (Answer)
B) Wolfgang Amadeus Mozart

14- What is the name of the famous American singer who is known for his smooth voice and songs like Fly Me to the Moon?
A) Frank Sinatra (Answer)
B) Dean Martin

15- What is the name of the famous British band that released the album OK Computer?
A) Radiohead (Answer)
B) Oasis

16- What is the name of the famous American singer who sang the song Toxic?
A) Britney Spears (Answer)
B) Christina Aguilera

17- What is the name of the famous composer who wrote the opera Carmen?
A) Georges Bizet (Answer)
B) Richard Wagner

18- What is the name of the famous American singer who is known for her unique voice and songs like Crazy?
A) Patsy Cline (Answer) B) Dolly Parton

19- What is the name of the famous British band that released the album Sgt. Pepper's Lonely Hearts Club Band?
A) The Beatles (Answer) B) The Rolling Stones

20- What is the name of the famous American singer who is known for her powerful voice and songs like Respect?
A) Aretha Franklin (Answer) B) Tina Turner

21- What is the name of the famous American band that released the album Nevermind?
A) Nirvana (Answer) B) Metallica

1- What is the name of the famous Chinese dish that is made with stir-fried noodles and vegetables?
A) Chow Mein
B) Pad Thai

2- What is the name of the famous Chinese dish that is made with steamed buns filled with meat and vegetables?
A) Baozi
B) Sushi

3- What is the name of the famous Chinese dish that is made with rice, vegetables, and meat or seafood?
A) Fried Rice
B) Paella

4- What is the name of the famous Chinese dish that is made with chicken and peanuts in a spicy sauce?
A) Kung Pao Chicken
B) General Tso's Chicken

5- What is the name of the famous Chinese dish that is made with dumplings filled with meat or vegetables?
A) Jiaozi
B) Samosas

6- What is the name of the famous Chinese dish that is made with egg noodles, roast pork, and vegetables in a soup?
A) Wonton Noodle Soup
B) Pho

7- What is the name of the famous Chinese dish that is made with shrimp, vegetables, and noodles in a clear broth?
A) Shrimp Wonton Soup
B) Miso Soup

8- What is the name of the famous Chinese dish that is made with fish filets and vegetables in a spicy broth?
A) Sichuan Hot Pot
B) Tom Yum Soup

9- What is the name of the famous Chinese dish that is made with steamed fish and vegetables in a soy sauce-based broth?
A) Steamed Fish
B) Fish and Chips

10- What is the name of the famous Chinese dish that is made with stir-fried vegetables and cashews?
A) Vegetarian Cashew Nut Stir Fry
B) Pad See Ew

11- What is the name of the famous Chinese dish that is made with spicy fried chicken and vegetables?
A) Chongqing Spicy Chicken
B) Buffalo Wings

12- What is the name of the famous Chinese dish that is made with deep-fried tofu in a spicy sauce?
A) Mapo Tofu
B) Falafel

13- What is the name of the famous Chinese dish that is made with fried rice noodles, beef, and vegetables?
A) Beef Chow Fun
B) Bibimbap

14- What is the name of the famous Chinese dish that is made with steamed rice and various toppings?
A) Congee
B) Risotto

15- What is the name of the famous Chinese dish that is made with stir-fried eggplant in a spicy sauce?
A) Yu Xiang Qie Zi
B) Ratatouille

16- What is the name of the famous Chinese dish that is made with stir-fried shrimp and vegetables in a spicy sauce?
A) Sichuan Spicy Shrimp
B) Shrimp Scampi

17- What is the name of the famous Chinese dish that is made with stir-fried beef and vegetables in a black bean sauce?
A) Beef with Black Bean Sauce
B) Beef Stroganoff

18- What is the name of the famous Chinese dish that is made with steamed buns filled with barbecued pork?
A) Char Siu Bao
B) Gyoza

ANSWERS

1- What is the name of the famous Chinese dish that is made with stir-fried noodles and vegetables?
A) Chow Mein (Answer)
B) Pad Thai

2- What is the name of the famous Chinese dish that is made with steamed buns filled with meat and vegetables?
A) Baozi (Answer)
B) Sushi

3- What is the name of the famous Chinese dish that is made with rice, vegetables, and meat or seafood?
A) Fried Rice (Answer)
B) Paella

4- What is the name of the famous Chinese dish that is made with chicken and peanuts in a spicy sauce?
A) Kung Pao Chicken (Answer)
B) General Tso's Chicken

5- What is the name of the famous Chinese dish that is made with dumplings filled with meat or vegetables?
A) Jiaozi (Answer)
B) Samosas

6- What is the name of the famous Chinese dish that is made with egg noodles, roast pork, and vegetables in a soup?
A) Wonton Noodle Soup (Answer)
B) Pho

7- What is the name of the famous Chinese dish that is made with shrimp, vegetables, and noodles in a clear broth?
A) Shrimp Wonton Soup (Answer)
B) Miso Soup

8- What is the name of the famous Chinese dish that is made with fish filets and vegetables in a spicy broth?
A) Sichuan Hot Pot (Answer)
B) Tom Yum Soup

9- What is the name of the famous Chinese dish that is made with steamed fish and vegetables in a soy sauce-based broth?
A) Steamed Fish (Answer)
B) Fish and Chips

10- What is the name of the famous Chinese dish that is made with stir-fried vegetables and cashews?
A) Vegetarian Cashew Nut Stir Fry (Answer)
B) Pad See Ew

11- What is the name of the famous Chinese dish that is made with spicy fried chicken and vegetables?
A) Chongqing Spicy Chicken (Answer)
B) Buffalo Wings

12- What is the name of the famous Chinese dish that is made with deep-fried tofu in a spicy sauce?
A) Mapo Tofu (Answer)
B) Falafel

13- What is the name of the famous Chinese dish that is made with fried rice noodles, beef, and vegetables?
A) Beef Chow Fun (Answer)
B) Bibimbap

14- What is the name of the famous Chinese dish that is made with steamed rice and various toppings?
A) Congee (Answer)
B) Risotto

15- What is the name of the famous Chinese dish that is made with stir-fried eggplant in a spicy sauce?
A) Yu Xiang Qie Zi (Answer)
B) Ratatouille

16- What is the name of the famous Chinese dish that is made with stir-fried shrimp and vegetables in a spicy sauce?
A) Sichuan Spicy Shrimp (Answer)
B) Shrimp Scampi

17- What is the name of the famous Chinese dish that is made with stir-fried beef and vegetables in a black bean sauce?
A) Beef with Black Bean Sauce (Answer)
B) Beef Stroganoff

18- What is the name of the famous Chinese dish that is made with steamed buns filled with barbecued pork?
A) Char Siu Bao (Answer)
B) Gyoza

Who is credited with inventing the electric car?
A) Thomas Edison
B) Robert Anderson

What is the term for the device used to recharge an electric car's batteries?
A) Charging station
B) Fuel pump

What is the name of the first commercially available electric car?
A) Tesla Roadster
B) GM EV1

What is the term for the process of converting stored energy in a battery into power to drive an electric car's motor?
A) Regenerative braking
B) Discharging

What is the name of the world's best-selling electric car model?
A) Nissan Leaf
B) Tesla Model S

What is the term for the maximum distance an electric car can travel on a single charge?
A) Range
B) Speed

What is the name of the company that produces the electric car model named after the famous inventor and scientist?
A) Edison Motors
B) Tesla Motors

What is the term for the system that allows an electric car's motor to operate in reverse to slow down the car and recharge the battery?
A) Regenerative braking
B) Forward regenerating

What is the term for a device that converts direct current (DC) from an electric car's battery to alternating current (AC) for use by the car's motor?
A) Inverter
B) Transformer

What is the name of the first electric car to exceed 300 miles on a single charge?
A) Tesla Model S
B) Chevrolet Bolt EV

What is the term for a type of electric car motor that uses permanent magnets instead of electromagnets?
A) Brushless DC motor
B) Induction motor

What is the name of the company that produces the Chevrolet Bolt EV?
A) General Motors
B) Ford Motors

What is the term for a type of electric car motor that uses electromagnets instead of permanent magnets?
A) Induction motor
B) Brushless DC motor

What is the name of the company that produces the Renault Zoe?
A) BMW
B) Renault

What is the term for the time required to recharge an electric car's battery to full capacity?
A) Charge time
B) Discharge time

What is the name of the electric car model produced by the luxury car brand Jaguar?
A) Jaguar XE
B) Jaguar I-PACE

What is the term for the process of converting mechanical energy from an electric car's motor into stored energy in its battery?
A) Charging
B) Regenerative braking

What is the name of the electric car model produced by the Korean automaker Hyundai?
A) Hyundai Kona Electric
B) Hyundai Tucson

What is the term for the device used to connect an electric car to a charging station?
A) Adapter B) Connector

What is the name of the company that produces the electric car model named after a famous scientist and inventor?
A) Edison Motors B) Tesla Motors

What is the term for the device used to connect an electric car's battery to a charger?
A) Charging port B) Fuel inlet

What is the name of the company that produces the electric car model named after the Greek word for "new"?
A) Nio B) Rivian

ANSWERS

Who is credited with inventing the electric car?
A) Thomas Edison
B) Robert Anderson (Answer)

What is the term for the device used to recharge an electric car's batteries?
A) Charging station (Answer)
B) Fuel pump

What is the name of the first commercially available electric car?
A) Tesla Roadster
B) GM EV1 (Answer)

What is the term for the process of converting stored energy in a battery into power to drive an electric car's motor?
A) Regenerative braking
B) Discharging (Answer)

What is the name of the world's best-selling electric car model?
A) Nissan Leaf (Answer)
B) Tesla Model S

What is the term for the maximum distance an electric car can travel on a single charge?
A) Range (Answer)
B) Speed

What is the name of the company that produces the electric car model named after the famous inventor and scientist?
A) Edison Motors
B) Tesla Motors (Answer)

What is the term for the system that allows an electric car's motor to operate in reverse to slow down the car and recharge the battery?
A) Regenerative braking (Answer)
B) Forward regenerating

What is the term for a device that converts direct current (DC) from an electric car's battery to alternating current (AC) for use by the car's motor?
A) Inverter (Answer)
B) Transformer

What is the name of the first electric car to exceed 300 miles on a single charge?
A) Tesla Model S (Answer)
B) Chevrolet Bolt EV

What is the term for a type of electric car motor that uses permanent magnets instead of electromagnets?
A) Brushless DC motor (Answer)
B) Induction motor

What is the name of the company that produces the Chevrolet Bolt EV?
A) General Motors (Answer)
B) Ford Motors

What is the term for a type of electric car motor that uses electromagnets instead of permanent magnets?
A) Induction motor (Answer)
B) Brushless DC motor

What is the name of the company that produces the Renault Zoe?
A) BMW
B) Renault (Answer)

What is the term for the time required to recharge an electric car's battery to full capacity?
A) Charge time (Answer)
B) Discharge time

What is the name of the electric car model produced by the luxury car brand Jaguar?
A) Jaguar XE
B) Jaguar I-PACE (Answer)

What is the term for the process of converting mechanical energy from an electric car's motor into stored energy in its battery?
A) Charging
B) Regenerative braking (Answer)

What is the name of the electric car model produced by the Korean automaker Hyundai?
A) Hyundai Kona Electric (Answer)
B) Hyundai Tucson

What is the term for the device used to connect an electric car to a charging station?
A) Adapter (Answer)
B) Connector

What is the name of the company that produces the electric car model named after a famous scientist and inventor?
A) Edison Motors B) Tesla Motors (Answer)

What is the term for the device used to connect an electric car's battery to a charger? A) Charging port (Answer) B) Fuel inlet

What is the name of the company that produces the electric car model named after the Greek word for "new"?
A) Nio (Answer) B) Rivian

What is the largest species of snake in the world?
A) Anaconda
B) Rattlesnake

What is the term for a group of snakes?
A) Swarm
B) Den

What is the name of the snake that can fly short distances by gliding through the air?
A) Flying viper
B) Flying cobra

What is the term for the process of shedding a snake's skin?
A) Sloughing
B) Molting

What is the name of the snake that can spit venom at its prey?
A) King cobra
B) Spitting cobra

What is the term for the triangular-shaped head of a venomous snake?
A) Arrowhead
B) Pit

What is the name of the snake that is known for its bright colors and patterns?
A) Rattlesnake
B) Coral snake

What is the term for the heat-sensing organs located on the head of a snake?
A) Echolocation
B) Pit organs

What is the name of the largest venomous snake in North America?
A) Copperhead
B) Diamondback rattlesnake

What is the term for the process of coiling around and suffocating prey?
A) Constricting
B) Strangling

What is the name of the snake that is known for its ability to climb trees?
A) Boa constrictor
B) Green tree python

What is the term for a venomous snake that does not have fangs?
A) Fangless snake
B) Rear-fanged snake

What is the name of the snake that is known for its ability to spit its venom with great accuracy?
A) Black mamba
B) Spitting cobra

What is the term for the snake's jaw that allows it to open its mouth wide enough to swallow prey whole?
A) Mandible
B) Quadrate bone

What is the name of the snake that is known for its ability to swim in the ocean?
A) Sea snake
B) Water moccasin

What is the term for a snake that gives birth to live young?
A) Oviparous
B) Viviparous

What is the name of the snake that is known for its ability to climb walls and ceilings?
A) Boa constrictor
B) Asian vine snake

What is the term for the scales on the underside of a snake's body?
A) Dorsal scales
B) Ventral scales

What is the name of the snake that is known for its ability to change color to match its surroundings?
A) Chameleon snake
B) Green tree python

What is the term for a snake that lays eggs?
A) Ovoviviparous
B) Oviparous

What is the name of the snake that is known for its ability to play dead when threatened?
A) King snake
B) Hognose snake

What is the term for the opening on a snake's head that it uses to smell its surroundings?
A) Olfactory bulb
B) Pit organ

What is the name of the snake that is known for its ability to spit its venom up to 10 feet away?
A) Cobra
B) Black-necked spitting cobra

ANSWERS

What is the largest species of snake in the world?
A) Anaconda (Answer)
B) Rattlesnake

What is the term for a group of snakes?
A) Swarm
B) Den (Answer)

What is the name of the snake that can fly short distances by gliding through the air?
A) Flying viper (Answer)
B) Flying cobra

What is the term for the process of shedding a snake's skin?
A) Sloughing (Answer)
B) Molting

What is the name of the snake that can spit venom at its prey?
A) King cobra
B) Spitting cobra (Answer)

What is the term for the triangular-shaped head of a venomous snake?
A) Arrowhead
B) Pit (Answer)

What is the name of the snake that is known for its bright colors and patterns?
A) Rattlesnake
B) Coral snake (Answer)

What is the term for the heat-sensing organs located on the head of a snake?
A) Echolocation
B) Pit organs (Answer)

What is the name of the largest venomous snake in North America?
A) Copperhead
B) Diamondback rattlesnake (Answer)

What is the term for the process of coiling around and suffocating prey?
A) Constricting (Answer)
B) Strangling

What is the name of the snake that is known for its ability to climb trees?
A) Boa constrictor
B) Green tree python (Answer)

What is the term for a venomous snake that does not have fangs?
A) Fangless snake
B) Rear-fanged snake (Answer)

What is the name of the snake that is known for its ability to spit its venom with great accuracy?
A) Black mamba
B) Spitting cobra (Answer)

What is the term for the snake's jaw that allows it to open its mouth wide enough to swallow prey whole?
A) Mandible
B) Quadrate bone (Answer)

What is the name of the snake that is known for its ability to swim in the ocean?
A) Sea snake (Answer)
B) Water moccasin

What is the term for a snake that gives birth to live young?
A) Oviparous
B) Viviparous (Answer)

What is the name of the snake that is known for its ability to climb walls and ceilings?
A) Boa constrictor
B) Asian vine snake (Answer)

What is the term for the scales on the underside of a snake's body?
A) Dorsal scales
B) Ventral scales (Answer)

What is the name of the snake that is known for its ability to change color to match its surroundings?
A) Chameleon snake
B) Green tree python (Answer)

What is the term for a snake that lays eggs?
A) Ovoviviparous
B) Oviparous (Answer)

What is the name of the snake that is known for its ability to play dead when threatened?
A) King snake
B) Hognose snake (Answer)

What is the term for the opening on a snake's head that it uses to smell its surroundings?
A) Olfactory bulb (Answer)
B) Pit organ

What is the name of the snake that is known for its ability to spit its venom up to 10 feet away?
A) Cobra
B) Black-necked spitting cobra (Answer)

1- When was the first US penny minted?
A) 1787
B) 1879

2- How much does a penny weigh?
A) 2.5 grams
B) 5 grams

3- What material are pennies made of?
A) Copper
B) Zinc

4- What president's portrait is on the penny?
A) George Washington
B) Abraham Lincoln

5- What is the diameter of a penny?
A) 19.05 mm
B) 25.4 mm

6- What is the value of a penny in cents?
A) 1
B) 10

7- What year did the Lincoln penny replace the Indian Head penny?
A) 1909
B) 1950

8- How many ridges are on the edge of a penny?
A) 118
B) 119

9- How many times can a penny be folded before it breaks?
A) 7
B) 10

10- How long is the average lifespan of a penny in circulation?
A) 25 years
B) 50 years

11- What animal is on the reverse side of the Lincoln penny?
A) Eagle
B) Shield

12- How many pennies are in a roll?
A) 40
B) 50

13- What is the most valuable penny ever sold?
A) 1943 copper penny
B) 1955 doubled die penny

14- What is the smallest denomination of US currency?
A) Penny
B) Nickel

15- What year did the US Mint start making steel pennies?
A) 1943
B) 1955

16- What is the most common year for Lincoln pennies?
A) 1958
B) 1982

17- Who designed the Lincoln penny?
A) James B. Longacre
B) Victor D. Brenner

18- How many pennies does it take to make a dollar?
A) 100
B) 50

19- What is the weight of 1000 pennies in pounds?
A) 2.5 lbs
B) 6.25 lbs

20- How many different designs of the Lincoln penny have been minted?
A) 4
B) 14

21- What is the largest penny ever made?
A) 3 feet in diameter
B) 1 foot in diameter

22- Can you still use pennies to pay for tolls on some highways?
A) Yes
B) No

23- How much does it cost to make a penny?
A) 0.5 cents
B) 1.5 cents

24- How many pennies would it take to make a tower as tall as the Empire State Building?
A) 10 million
B) 100 billion

ANSWERS

1- When was the first US penny minted?
A) 1787 (Answer)
B) 1879

2- How much does a penny weigh?
A) 2.5 grams (Answer)
B) 5 grams

3- What material are pennies made of?
A) Copper (Answer)
B) Zinc

4- What president's portrait is on the penny?
A) George Washington (Answer)
B) Abraham Lincoln

5- What is the diameter of a penny?
A) 19.05 mm (Answer)
B) 25.4 mm

6- What is the value of a penny in cents?
A) 1 (Answer)
B) 10

7- What year did the Lincoln penny replace the Indian Head penny?
A) 1909 (Answer)
B) 1950

8- How many ridges are on the edge of a penny?
A) 118
B) 119 (Answer)

9- How many times can a penny be folded before it breaks?
A) 7
B) 10 (Answer)

10- How long is the average lifespan of a penny in circulation?
A) 25 years (Answer)
B) 50 years

11- What animal is on the reverse side of the Lincoln penny?
A) Eagle
B) Shield (Answer)

12- How many pennies are in a roll?
A) 40
B) 50 (Answer)

13- What is the most valuable penny ever sold?
A) 1943 copper penny (Answer)
B) 1955 doubled die penny

14- What is the smallest denomination of US currency?
A) Penny (Answer)
B) Nickel

15- What year did the US Mint start making steel pennies?
A) 1943 (Answer)
B) 1955

16- What is the most common year for Lincoln pennies?
A) 1958
B) 1982 (Answer)

17- Who designed the Lincoln penny?
A) James B. Longacre
B) Victor D. Brenner (Answer)

18- How many pennies does it take to make a dollar?
A) 100 (Answer)
B) 50

19- What is the weight of 1000 pennies in pounds?
A) 2.5 lbs
B) 6.25 lbs (Answer)

20- How many different designs of the Lincoln penny have been minted?
A) 4
B) 14 (Answer)

21- What is the largest penny ever made?
A) 3 feet in diameter (Answer)
B) 1 foot in diameter

22- Can you still use pennies to pay for tolls on some highways?
A) Yes (Answer)
B) No

23- How much does it cost to make a penny?
A) 0.5 cents
B) 1.5 cents (Answer)

24- How many pennies would it take to make a tower as tall as the Empire State Building?
A) 10 million
B) 100 billion (Answer)

1- What is the name of the iconic video game character that first appeared in 1981 and loves to eat dots and fruit?
A) Mario
B) Pac-Man

2- What is the name of the popular video game franchise featuring characters such as Master Chief and Cortana?
A) Call of Duty
B) Halo

3- What is the name of the popular video game that features a world made of blocks and allows players to build and explore their own creations?
A) Minecraft
B) Terraria

4- What is the name of the classic arcade game where players control a spaceship and shoot down waves of aliens?
A) Galaga
B) Space Invaders

5- What is the name of the popular video game series that has players battle against hordes of zombies?
A) Resident Evil
B) Left 4 Dead

6- What is the name of the video game that features a plumber named Mario who tries to rescue a princess from a giant turtle named Bowser?
A) Sonic the Hedgehog
B) Super Mario Bros.

7- What is the name of the video game that features a hedgehog named Sonic who runs and jumps through various levels to stop Dr. Eggman?
A) Sonic Heroes
B) Sonic the Hedgehog

8- What is the name of the video game franchise that allows players to race as their favorite characters on different tracks?
A) Need for Speed
B) Mario Kart

9- What is the name of the popular video game franchise that features characters such as Solid Snake and Big Boss?
A) Metal Gear Solid
B) Splinter Cell

10- What is the name of the popular video game series that features a group of Italian-American plumbers who go on adventures in a fantasy world?
A) Super Mario Bros.
B) Luigi's Mansion

11- What is the name of the video game franchise that has players control a character named Nathan Drake as he goes on treasure hunting adventures?
A) Tomb Raider
B) Uncharted

12- What is the name of the video game that allows players to create and control their own virtual people in a simulated world?
A) The Sims
B) SimCity

13- What is the name of the video game franchise that features characters such as Scorpion and Sub-Zero battling it out in a fighting tournament?
A) Tekken
B) Mortal Kombat

14- What is the name of the video game that has players control a character named Link as he goes on adventures to rescue Princess Zelda?
A) The Legend of Zelda
B) Final Fantasy

15- What is the name of the video game franchise that allows players to control different characters with unique abilities in a first-person shooter game?
A) Overwatch
B) Counter-Strike

16- What is the name of the popular video game that has players control a character named Kratos as he battles Greek gods and monsters?
A) God of War
B) Diablo

17- What is the name of the video game franchise that features different professions such as warrior, mage, and rogue as players embark on adventures in a fantasy world?
A) World of Warcraft
B) Elder Scrolls

18- What is the name of the video game franchise that allows players to build and manage their own amusement park?
A) Roller Coaster Tycoon
B) Theme Park

ANSWERS

1- What is the name of the iconic video game character that first appeared in 1981 and loves to eat dots and fruit?
A) Mario
B) Pac-Man (Answer)

2- What is the name of the popular video game franchise featuring characters such as Master Chief and Cortana?
A) Call of Duty
B) Halo (Answer)

3- What is the name of the popular video game that features a world made of blocks and allows players to build and explore their own creations?
A) Minecraft (Answer)
B) Terraria

4- What is the name of the classic arcade game where players control a spaceship and shoot down waves of aliens?
A) Galaga (Answer)
B) Space Invaders

5- What is the name of the popular video game series that has players battle against hordes of zombies?
A) Resident Evil
B) Left 4 Dead (Answer)

6- What is the name of the video game that features a plumber named Mario who tries to rescue a princess from a giant turtle named Bowser?
A) Sonic the Hedgehog
B) Super Mario Bros. (Answer)

7- What is the name of the video game that features a hedgehog named Sonic who runs and jumps through various levels to stop Dr. Eggman?
A) Sonic Heroes
B) Sonic the Hedgehog (Answer)

8- What is the name of the video game franchise that allows players to race as their favorite characters on different tracks?
A) Need for Speed
B) Mario Kart (Answer)

9- What is the name of the popular video game franchise that features characters such as Solid Snake and Big Boss?
A) Metal Gear Solid (Answer)
B) Splinter Cell

10- What is the name of the popular video game series that features a group of Italian-American plumbers who go on adventures in a fantasy world?
A) Super Mario Bros. (Answer)
B) Luigi's Mansion

11- What is the name of the video game franchise that has players control a character named Nathan Drake as he goes on treasure hunting adventures?
A) Tomb Raider
B) Uncharted (Answer)

12- What is the name of the video game that allows players to create and control their own virtual people in a simulated world?
A) The Sims (Answer)
B) SimCity

13- What is the name of the video game franchise that features characters such as Scorpion and Sub-Zero battling it out in a fighting tournament?
A) Tekken
B) Mortal Kombat (Answer)

14- What is the name of the video game that has players control a character named Link as he goes on adventures to rescue Princess Zelda?
A) The Legend of Zelda (Answer)
B) Final Fantasy

15- What is the name of the video game franchise that allows players to control different characters with unique abilities in a first-person shooter game?
A) Overwatch (Answer)
B) Counter-Strike

16- What is the name of the popular video game that has players control a character named Kratos as he battles Greek gods and monsters?
A) God of War (Answer)
B) Diablo

17- What is the name of the video game franchise that features different professions such as warrior, mage, and rogue as players embark on adventures in a fantasy world?
A) World of Warcraft (Answer)
B) Elder Scrolls

18- What is the name of the video game franchise that allows players to build and manage their own amusement park?
A) Roller Coaster Tycoon (Answer)
B) Theme Park

1- What is the world's tallest species of tree?
A) Redwood
B) Oak

2- What is the world's largest species of tree?
A) Giant Sequoia
B) Banyan

3- What is the smallest species of tree?
A) Dwarf Willow
B) Japanese Maple

4- How many species of trees are there in the world?
A) 10,000
B) 100,000

5- What is the name of the process that allows trees to convert sunlight into energy?
A) Photosynthesis
B) Respiration

6- What is the oldest species of tree?
A) Bristlecone Pine
B) Ginkgo Biloba

7- What is the most common species of tree in North America?
A) Oak
B) Red Maple

8- What is the most common species of tree in the world?
A) Pine
B) Eucalyptus

9- What is the largest tree in the Amazon Rainforest?
A) Kapok
B) Mahogany

10- What is the largest living organism on Earth?
A) Blue Whale
B) Giant Sequoia Tree

11- How many rings does it take to identify the age of a tree?
A) 1
B) Many

12- What is the fastest growing species of tree?
A) Eucalyptus
B) Bamboo

13- How long does it take for a tree to produce its first seed?
A) 1 year
B) 10 years

14- What is the average lifespan of a tree?
A) 50-100 years
B) 100-500 years

15- How many leaves can a mature oak tree produce?
A) 10,000
B) 500,000

16- What is the most expensive species of tree?
A) Teak
B) Cedar

17- What is the most endangered species of tree?
A) Redwood
B) Baobab

18- How tall can a mature Douglas Fir grow?
A) 50-75 feet
B) 200-300 feet

19- What is the most common tree in the African savanna?
A) Acacia
B) Baobab

20- What is the world's heaviest species of tree?
A) Sequoia
B) Oak

21- What is the most common tree in the rainforest?
A) Mahogany
B) Kapok

22- What is the state tree of California?
A) Redwood
B) Pine

23- What is the most widely planted species of tree in the world?
A) Pine
B) Eucalyptus

24- How much oxygen does one mature tree produce in a year?
A) Enough for 100 people
B) Enough for two people

25- What is the most widely recognized symbol of Arbor Day?
A) Tree planting
B) Tree cutting

ANSWERS

1- What is the world's tallest species of tree?
A) Redwood (Answer)
B) Oak

2- What is the world's largest species of tree?
A) Giant Sequoia (Answer)
B) Banyan

3- What is the smallest species of tree?
A) Dwarf Willow (Answer)
B) Japanese Maple

4- How many species of trees are there in the world?
A) 10,000
B) 100,000 (Answer)

5- What is the name of the process that allows trees to convert sunlight into energy?
A) Photosynthesis (Answer)
B) Respiration

6- What is the oldest species of tree?
A) Bristlecone Pine (Answer)
B) Ginkgo Biloba

7- What is the most common species of tree in North America?
A) Oak
B) Red Maple (Answer)

8- What is the most common species of tree in the world?
A) Pine
B) Eucalyptus (Answer)

9- What is the largest tree in the Amazon Rainforest?
A) Kapok (Answer)
B) Mahogany

10- What is the largest living organism on Earth?
A) Blue Whale
B) Giant Sequoia Tree (Answer)

11- How many rings does it take to identify the age of a tree?
A) 1
B) Many (Answer)

12- What is the fastest growing species of tree?
A) Eucalyptus (Answer)
B) Bamboo

13- How long does it take for a tree to produce its first seed?
A) 1 year
B) 10 years (Answer)

14- What is the average lifespan of a tree?
A) 50-100 years
B) 100-500 years (Answer)

15- How many leaves can a mature oak tree produce?
A) 10,000
B) 500,000 (Answer)

16- What is the most expensive species of tree?
A) Teak (Answer)
B) Cedar

17- What is the most endangered species of tree?
A) Redwood
B) Baobab (Answer)

18- How tall can a mature Douglas Fir grow?
A) 50-75 feet
B) 200-300 feet (Answer)

19- What is the most common tree in the African savanna?
A) Acacia (Answer)
B) Baobab

20- What is the world's heaviest species of tree?
A) Sequoia
B) Oak (Answer)

21- What is the most common tree in the rainforest?
A) Mahogany
B) Kapok (Answer)

22- What is the state tree of California?
A) Redwood (Answer)
B) Pine

23- What is the most widely planted species of tree in the world?
A) Pine
B) Eucalyptus (Answer)

24- How much oxygen does one mature tree produce in a year?
A) Enough for 100 people
B) Enough for two people (Answer)

25- What is the most widely recognized symbol of Arbor Day?
A) Tree planting (Answer)
B) Tree cutting

1- What is the name of the brightly colored fish that is often kept in aquariums?
A) Betta fish
B) Goldfish

2- What is the name of the tropical fish that is known for its ability to swim upside down?
A) Upside-down catfish
B) Angelfish

3- What is the name of the tropical fish that is known for its ability to change colors?
A) Rainbow fish
B) Neon tetra

4- What is the name of the tropical fish that is known for its ability to camouflage itself to match its surroundings?
A) Chameleon fish
B) Discus fish

5- What is the name of the tropical fish that is known for its sharp teeth and aggressive behavior?
A) Piranha
B) Clownfish

6- What is the name of the tropical fish that is known for its long, flowing fins?
A) Guppy
B) Siamese fighting fish

7- What is the name of the tropical fish that is known for its ability to jump out of the water?
A) Flying fish
B) Pufferfish

8- What is the name of the tropical fish that is known for its ability to mimic other fish and creatures?
A) Mimic octopus
B) Mimic blenny

9- What is the name of the tropical fish that is known for its bright yellow color?
A) Yellow tang
B) Blue tang

10- What is the name of the tropical fish that is known for its ability to create a symbiotic relationship with sea anemones?
A) Clownfish
B) Triggerfish

11- What is the name of the tropical fish that is known for its ability to inflate its body when threatened?
A) Pufferfish
B) Lionfish

12- What is the name of the tropical fish that is known for its ability to produce an electric shock?
A) Electric eel
B) Electric catfish

13- What is the name of the tropical fish that is known for its ability to change gender?
A) Clownfish
B) Bluehead wrasse

14- What is the name of the tropical fish that is known for its bright blue color and red tail?
A) Blue tang
B) Flame angelfish

15- What is the name of the tropical fish that is known for its ability to walk on land?
A) Mudskipper
B) Archerfish

16- What is the name of the tropical fish that is known for its ability to camouflage itself by changing the color of its eyes?
A) Cuttlefish
B) Stonefish

17- What is the name of the tropical fish that is known for its ability to create a symbiotic relationship with cleaner shrimp?
A) Goby
B) Tang

18- What is the name of the tropical fish that is known for its ability to make grunting sounds?
A) Gruntfish
B) Butterflyfish

19- What is the name of the tropical fish that is known for its ability to make clicking sounds?
A) Clicking goby
B) Triggerfish

20- What is the name of the tropical fish that is known for its ability to change its shape and appearance to mimic other fish?
A) Scorpionfish
B) Mimic octopus

21- What is the name of the tropical fish that is known for its ability to produce a venomous sting?
A) Stingray
B) Catfish

ANSWERS

1- What is the name of the brightly colored fish that is often kept in aquariums?
A) Betta fish (Answer)
B) Goldfish

2- What is the name of the tropical fish that is known for its ability to swim upside down?
A) Upside-down catfish (Answer)
B) Angelfish

3- What is the name of the tropical fish that is known for its ability to change colors?
A) Rainbow fish (Answer)
B) Neon tetra

4- What is the name of the tropical fish that is known for its ability to camouflage itself to match its surroundings?
A) Chameleon fish (Answer)
B) Discus fish

5- What is the name of the tropical fish that is known for its sharp teeth and aggressive behavior?
A) Piranha (Answer)
B) Clownfish

6- What is the name of the tropical fish that is known for its long, flowing fins?
A) Guppy
B) Siamese fighting fish (Answer)

7- What is the name of the tropical fish that is known for its ability to jump out of the water?
A) Flying fish (Answer)
B) Pufferfish

8- What is the name of the tropical fish that is known for its ability to mimic other fish and creatures?
A) Mimic octopus
B) Mimic blenny (Answer)

9- What is the name of the tropical fish that is known for its bright yellow color?
A) Yellow tang (Answer)
B) Blue tang

10- What is the name of the tropical fish that is known for its ability to create a symbiotic relationship with sea anemones?
A) Clownfish (Answer)
B) Triggerfish

11- What is the name of the tropical fish that is known for its ability to inflate its body when threatened?
A) Pufferfish (Answer)
B) Lionfish

12- What is the name of the tropical fish that is known for its ability to produce an electric shock?
A) Electric eel
B) Electric catfish (Answer)

13- What is the name of the tropical fish that is known for its ability to change gender?
A) Clownfish
B) Bluehead wrasse (Answer)

14- What is the name of the tropical fish that is known for its bright blue color and red tail?
A) Blue tang
B) Flame angelfish (Answer)

15- What is the name of the tropical fish that is known for its ability to walk on land?
A) Mudskipper (Answer)
B) Archerfish

16- What is the name of the tropical fish that is known for its ability to camouflage itself by changing the color of its eyes?
A) Cuttlefish
B) Stonefish (Answer)

17- What is the name of the tropical fish that is known for its ability to create a symbiotic relationship with cleaner shrimp?
A) Goby (Answer)
B) Tang

18- What is the name of the tropical fish that is known for its ability to make grunting sounds?
A) Gruntfish (Answer) B) Butterflyfish

19- What is the name of the tropical fish that is known for its ability to make clicking sounds?
A) Clicking goby (Answer) B) Triggerfish

20- What is the name of the tropical fish that is known for its ability to change its shape and appearance to mimic other fish?
A) Scorpionfish B) Mimic octopus (Answer)

21- What is the name of the tropical fish that is known for its ability to produce a venomous sting?
A) Stingray (Answer) B) Catfish

1- What is the name of the annual championship game of the National Football League?
A) Super Bowl
B) World Series

2- Which NFL team has won the most Super Bowl championships in history?
A) New England Patriots
B) Dallas Cowboys

3- What is the name of the stadium where the Dallas Cowboys play their home games?
A) AT&T Stadium
B) Mercedes-Benz Stadium

4- Which position is responsible for throwing the football and leading the team's offense?
A) Quarterback
B) Wide receiver

5- What is the name of the college football championship game?
A) College Football Playoff National Championship
B) BCS Championship

6- Which famous NFL quarterback holds the record for the most career touchdown passes?
A) Tom Brady
B) Joe Montana

7- What is the name of the trophy awarded to the winner of the Super Bowl?
A) Lombardi Trophy
B) Stanley Cup

8- Which NFL team won the first-ever Super Bowl championship in 1967?
A) Green Bay Packers
B) Pittsburgh Steelers

9- What is the name of the annual college football game between the Army and Navy?
A) Army-Navy Game
B) Iron Bowl

10- Which position is responsible for kicking field goals and extra points in football?
A) Kicker
B) Linebacker

11- What is the name of the professional football league that is played in the spring and features players who were not drafted or signed by NFL teams?
A) XFL
B) CFL

12- Which NFL team has the most regular-season wins in history?
A) Chicago Bears
B) Dallas Cowboys

13- What is the name of the annual college football game between the Michigan Wolverines and Ohio State Buckeyes?
A) The Game
B) Red River Rivalry

14- What is the name of the trophy awarded to the winner of the college football national championship game?
A) College Football Playoff National Championship Trophy
B) Heisman Trophy

15- Which famous NFL coach holds the record for the most career wins by a head coach?
A) Don Shula
B) Bill Belichick

16- What is the name of the professional football league that was founded in 1920 and is now known as the NFL?
A) American Football League
B) National Football League

17- What is the name of the annual college football game between the Alabama Crimson Tide and Auburn Tigers?
A) Iron Bowl
B) Red River Rivalry

18- Which NFL team won the most recent Super Bowl championship?
A) Tampa Bay Buccaneers
B) Kansas City Chiefs

19- What is the name of the annual college football game between the USC Trojans and UCLA Bruins?
A) Crosstown Classic
B) Bedlam Series

20- Which NFL team has the most appearances in the Super Bowl?
A) New England Patriots
B) Pittsburgh Steelers

21- What is the name of the trophy awarded to the winner of the Heisman Trophy?
A) Heisman Trophy
B) Lombardi Trophy

22- Which NFL team has the most regular-season losses in history?
A) Cleveland Browns B) Detroit Lions

ANSWERS

1- What is the name of the annual championship game of the National Football League?
A) Super Bowl (Answer)
B) World Series

2- Which NFL team has won the most Super Bowl championships in history?
A) New England Patriots (Answer)
B) Dallas Cowboys

3- What is the name of the stadium where the Dallas Cowboys play their home games?
A) AT&T Stadium (Answer)
B) Mercedes-Benz Stadium

4- Which position is responsible for throwing the football and leading the team's offense?
A) Quarterback (Answer)
B) Wide receiver

5- What is the name of the college football championship game?
A) College Football Playoff National Championship (Answer)
B) BCS Championship

6- Which famous NFL quarterback holds the record for the most career touchdown passes?
A) Tom Brady (Answer)
B) Joe Montana

7- What is the name of the trophy awarded to the winner of the Super Bowl?
A) Lombardi Trophy (Answer)
B) Stanley Cup

8- Which NFL team won the first-ever Super Bowl championship in 1967?
A) Green Bay Packers (Answer)
B) Pittsburgh Steelers

9- What is the name of the annual college football game between the Army and Navy?
A) Army-Navy Game (Answer)
B) Iron Bowl

10- Which position is responsible for kicking field goals and extra points in football?
A) Kicker (Answer)
B) Linebacker

11- What is the name of the professional football league that is played in the spring and features players who were not drafted or signed by NFL teams?
A) XFL (Answer)
B) CFL

12- Which NFL team has the most regular-season wins in history?
A) Chicago Bears
B) Dallas Cowboys (Answer)

13- What is the name of the annual college football game between the Michigan Wolverines and Ohio State Buckeyes?
A) The Game (Answer)
B) Red River Rivalry

14- What is the name of the trophy awarded to the winner of the college football national championship game?
A) College Football Playoff National Championship Trophy (Answer)
B) Heisman Trophy

15- Which famous NFL coach holds the record for the most career wins by a head coach?
A) Don Shula (Answer)
B) Bill Belichick

16- What is the name of the professional football league that was founded in 1920 and is now known as the NFL?
A) American Football League
B) National Football League (Answer)

17- What is the name of the annual college football game between the Alabama Crimson Tide and Auburn Tigers?
A) Iron Bowl (Answer)
B) Red River Rivalry

18- Which NFL team won the most recent Super Bowl championship?
A) Tampa Bay Buccaneers (Answer)
B) Kansas City Chiefs

19- What is the name of the annual college football game between the USC Trojans and UCLA Bruins?
A) Crosstown Classic (Answer)
B) Bedlam Series

20- Which NFL team has the most appearances in the Super Bowl?
A) New England Patriots (Answer)
B) Pittsburgh Steelers

21- What is the name of the trophy awarded to the winner of the Heisman Trophy?
A) Heisman Trophy (Answer) B) Lombardi Trophy

22- Which NFL team has the most regular-season losses in history?
A) Cleveland Browns (Answer) B) Detroit Lions

1- What is the name of the famous ancient Egyptian pharaoh who ruled during the 18th dynasty?
A) King Tutankhamun
B) Ramses II

2- What is the name of the ancient Egyptian goddess of fertility and motherhood?
A) Isis
B) Bastet

3- What is the name of the ancient Egyptian capital city that is now known as Luxor?
A) Thebes
B) Memphis

4- What is the name of the ancient Egyptian writing system that used pictures to represent words and ideas?
A) Hieroglyphics
B) Cuneiform

5- What is the name of the famous ancient Egyptian queen who was known for her beauty and her political influence?
A) Nefertiti
B) Cleopatra

6- What is the name of the ancient Egyptian god of the afterlife who was often depicted with the head of a jackal?
A) Anubis
B) Horus

7- What is the name of the ancient Egyptian god of the sun who was often depicted as a falcon?
A) Ra
B) Osiris

8- What is the name of the ancient Egyptian festival that celebrated the flooding of the Nile River?
A) Opet
B) Festival of Osiris

9- What is the name of the ancient Egyptian queen who was the wife of King Akhenaten and mother of King Tutankhamun?
A) Nefertiti
B) Hatshepsut

10- What is the name of the ancient Egyptian god of the underworld who was often depicted as a man with a jackal's head?
A) Anubis
B) Thoth

11- What is the name of the ancient Egyptian god of wisdom and writing who was often depicted as a man with the head of an ibis?
A) Thoth
B) Ptah

12- What is the name of the ancient Egyptian god of the desert who was often depicted as a man with the head of a falcon?
A) Horus
B) Set

13- What is the name of the ancient Egyptian queen who ruled during the New Kingdom and is famous for her monumental building projects?
A) Hatshepsut
B) Nefertiti

14- What is the name of the ancient Egyptian god of the Nile River who was often depicted as a man with a head of a crocodile?
A) Sobek
B) Anubis

15- What is the name of the ancient Egyptian queen who ruled as a pharaoh and is known for her distinctive female beard?
A) Hatshepsut
B) Nefertiti

16- What is the name of the ancient Egyptian god of fertility who was often depicted with a phallus?
A) Min
B) Amun

17- What is the name of the ancient Egyptian god of chaos and disorder who was often depicted as a serpent?
A) Apophis
B) Set

18- What is the name of the ancient Egyptian festival that celebrated the rebirth of the god Osiris?
A) Festival of Osiris
B) Opet

19- What is the name of the ancient Egyptian god of the sky who was often depicted as a man with the head of a falcon?
A) Horus
B) Ra

ANSWERS

1- What is the name of the famous ancient Egyptian pharaoh who ruled during the 18th dynasty?
A) King Tutankhamun
B) Ramses II (Answer)

2- What is the name of the ancient Egyptian goddess of fertility and motherhood?
A) Isis (Answer)
B) Bastet

3- What is the name of the ancient Egyptian capital city that is now known as Luxor?
A) Thebes (Answer)
B) Memphis

4- What is the name of the ancient Egyptian writing system that used pictures to represent words and ideas?
A) Hieroglyphics (Answer)
B) Cuneiform

5- What is the name of the famous ancient Egyptian queen who was known for her beauty and her political influence?
A) Nefertiti (Answer)
B) Cleopatra

6- What is the name of the ancient Egyptian god of the afterlife who was often depicted with the head of a jackal?
A) Anubis (Answer)
B) Horus

7- What is the name of the ancient Egyptian god of the sun who was often depicted as a falcon?
A) Ra (Answer)
B) Osiris

8- What is the name of the ancient Egyptian festival that celebrated the flooding of the Nile River?
A) Opet (Answer)
B) Festival of Osiris

9- What is the name of the ancient Egyptian queen who was the wife of King Akhenaten and mother of King Tutankhamun?
A) Nefertiti (Answer)
B) Hatshepsut

10- What is the name of the ancient Egyptian god of the underworld who was often depicted as a man with a jackal's head?
A) Anubis (Answer)
B) Thoth

11- What is the name of the ancient Egyptian god of wisdom and writing who was often depicted as a man with the head of an ibis?
A) Thoth (Answer)
B) Ptah

12- What is the name of the ancient Egyptian god of the desert who was often depicted as a man with the head of a falcon?
A) Horus
B) Set (Answer)

13- What is the name of the ancient Egyptian queen who ruled during the New Kingdom and is famous for her monumental building projects?
A) Hatshepsut (Answer)
B) Nefertiti

14- What is the name of the ancient Egyptian god of the Nile River who was often depicted as a man with a head of a crocodile?
A) Sobek (Answer)
B) Anubis

15- What is the name of the ancient Egyptian queen who ruled as a pharaoh and is known for her distinctive female beard?
A) Hatshepsut (Answer)
B) Nefertiti

16- What is the name of the ancient Egyptian god of fertility who was often depicted with a phallus?
A) Min (Answer)
B) Amun

17- What is the name of the ancient Egyptian god of chaos and disorder who was often depicted as a serpent?
A) Apophis (Answer)
B) Set

18- What is the name of the ancient Egyptian festival that celebrated the rebirth of the god Osiris?
A) Festival of Osiris (Answer)
B) Opet

19- What is the name of the ancient Egyptian god of the sky who was often depicted as a man with the head of a falcon?
A) Horus (Answer)
B) Ra

1- Who is considered to be the "King of the Blues" and plays a famous guitar named "Lucille"?
A) B.B. King
B) Jimi Hendrix

2- What type of guitar is typically used to play flamenco music?
A) Classical guitar
B) Electric guitar

3- What type of guitar did Eddie Van Halen famously play?
A) Stratocaster
B) Frankenstrat

4- What is the name of the part of a guitar that is used to adjust the tension of the strings?
A) Tuning pegs
B) Bridge

5- What type of guitar is typically used to play heavy metal music?
A) Acoustic guitar
B) Electric guitar

6- What is the name of the company that produces the Les Paul guitar?
A) Fender
B) Gibson

7- What is the name of the technique used to create a percussive sound on the guitar by tapping the strings with the fingers or hand?
A) Fingerstyle
B) Percussive tapping

8- What is the term for the device used to amplify the sound of an electric guitar?
A) Amplifier
B) Equalizer

9- What type of guitar is typically used to play country music?
A) Classical guitar
B) Acoustic guitar

10- What is the name of the device used to bend the pitch of a guitar string?
A) Wah pedal
B) Whammy bar

11- What type of guitar did Jimi Hendrix famously play?
A) Stratocaster
B) Les Paul

12- What is the name of the technique used to play two notes at once on the guitar by plucking the strings with both hands?
A) Tapping
B) Two-handed tapping

13- What is the term for the device used to produce a distortion effect on the sound of an electric guitar?
A) Overdrive pedal
B) Distortion pedal

14- What type of guitar is typically used to play jazz music?
A) Electric guitar
B) Archtop guitar

15- What is the name of the part of a guitar that is used to press down the strings against the frets?
A) Fretboard
B) Neck

16- What is the term for the device used to produce a chorus effect on the sound of an electric guitar?
A) Chorus pedal
B) Flanger pedal

17- What type of guitar is typically used to play classical music?
A) Archtop guitar
B) Classical guitar

18- What is the name of the part of a guitar that is used to support the strings and transfer their vibrations to the body of the guitar?
A) Bridge
B) Saddle

19- What type of guitar is typically used to play blues music?
A) Acoustic guitar
B) Electric guitar

20- What is the name of the device used to produce a delay effect on the sound of an electric guitar?
A) Delay pedal
B) Reverb pedal

21- What is the term for the device used to produce a wah-wah effect on the sound of an electric guitar?
A) Whammy bar
B) Wah pedal

22- What type of guitar is typically used to play rock music?
A) Acoustic guitar
B) Electric guitar

23- What is the name of the part of a guitar that is used to adjust the height of the strings from the fretboard?
A) Nut
B) Truss rod

ANSWERS

1- Who is considered to be the "King of the Blues" and played a famous guitar named "Lucille"?
A) B.B. King (Answer)
B) Jimi Hendrix

2- What type of guitar is typically used to play flamenco music?
A) Classical guitar (Answer)
B) Electric guitar

3- What type of guitar did Eddie Van Halen famously play?
A) Stratocaster
B) Frankenstrat (Answer)

4- What is the name of the part of a guitar that is used to adjust the tension of the strings?
A) Tuning pegs (Answer)
B) Bridge

5- What type of guitar is typically used to play heavy metal music?
A) Acoustic guitar
B) Electric guitar (Answer)

6- What is the name of the company that produces the Les Paul guitar?
A) Fender
B) Gibson (Answer)

7- What is the name of the technique used to create a percussive sound on the guitar by tapping the strings with the fingers or hand?
A) Fingerstyle
B) Percussive tapping (Answer)

8- What is the term for the device used to amplify the sound of an electric guitar?
A) Amplifier (Answer)
B) Equalizer

9- What type of guitar is typically used to play country music?
A) Classical guitar
B) Acoustic guitar (Answer)

10- What is the name of the device used to bend the pitch of a guitar string?
A) Wah pedal
B) Whammy bar (Answer)

11- What type of guitar did Jimi Hendrix famously play?
A) Stratocaster (Answer)
B) Les Paul

12- What is the name of the technique used to play two notes at once on the guitar by plucking the strings with both hands?
A) Tapping
B) Two-handed tapping (Answer)

13- What is the term for the device used to produce a distortion effect on the sound of an electric guitar?
A) Overdrive pedal
B) Distortion pedal (Answer)

14- What type of guitar is typically used to play jazz music?
A) Electric guitar
B) Archtop guitar (Answer)

15- What is the name of the part of a guitar that is used to press down the strings against the frets?
A) Fretboard (Answer)
B) Neck

16- What is the term for the device used to produce a chorus effect on the sound of an electric guitar?
A) Chorus pedal (Answer)
B) Flanger pedal

17- What type of guitar is typically used to play classical music?
A) Archtop guitar
B) Classical guitar (Answer)

18- What is the name of the part of a guitar that is used to support the strings and transfer their vibrations to the body of the guitar?
A) Bridge (Answer)
B) Saddle

19- What type of guitar is typically used to play blues music?
A) Acoustic guitar
B) Electric guitar (Answer)

20- What is the name of the device used to produce a delay effect on the sound of an electric guitar?
A) Delay pedal (Answer)
B) Reverb pedal

21- What is the term for the device used to produce a wah-wah effect on the sound of an electric guitar?
A) Whammy bar
B) Wah pedal (Answer)

22- What type of guitar is typically used to play rock music?
A) Acoustic guitar
B) Electric guitar (Answer)

23- What is the name of the part of a guitar that is used to adjust the height of the strings from the fretboard?
A) Nut
B) Truss rod (Answer)

1- Who was the Queen of England during World War II?
A) Queen Elizabeth II
B) Queen Elizabeth, the Queen Mother

2- Who was the first female pharaoh of ancient Egypt?
A) Nefertiti
B) Hatshepsut

3- Who was the Queen of France during the French Revolution?
A) Marie Antoinette
B) Catherine the Great

4- Who was the Queen of Spain during the 16th century who supported Christopher Columbus' voyage to the Americas?
A) Isabella I
B) Maria Theresa

5- Who was the Queen of Scotland who was executed by Queen Elizabeth I of England?
A) Mary, Queen of Scots
B) Catherine of Aragon

6- Who was the Queen of England who ruled from 1558 to 1603 and oversaw a period of great cultural and economic growth?
A) Queen Victoria
B) Queen Elizabeth I

7- Who was the Queen of Egypt who ruled during the Ptolemaic dynasty and was known for her beauty and intelligence?
A) Cleopatra
B) Nefertiti

8- Who was the Queen of Sheba who visited King Solomon in the Bible?
A) Queen Esther
B) Queen of Sheba

9- Who was the Queen of England who ruled from 1837 to 1901 and oversaw a period of great industrial expansion and colonialism?
A) Queen Elizabeth II
B) Queen Victoria

10- Who was the Queen of England who was famously beheaded by her husband King Henry VIII?
A) Anne Boleyn
B) Mary, Queen of Scots

11- Who was the Queen of Spain who supported the famous painter Diego Velázquez?
A) Isabella II
B) Isabella I

12- Who was the Queen of England who ruled from 1603 to 1625 and sponsored the arts and literature during the Elizabethan era?
A) Queen Mary I
B) Queen Elizabeth I

13- Who was the Queen of England who ruled from 1702 to 1714 and oversaw the War of the Spanish Succession?
A) Queen Anne
B) Queen Victoria

14- Who was the Queen of England who was known as the "Virgin Queen" because she never married?
A) Queen Elizabeth I
B) Queen Mary I

15- Who was the Queen of England who was known for her philanthropy and charity work, and ruled during the 19th century?
A) Queen Elizabeth II
B) Queen Victoria

16- Who was the Queen of France who was married to King Louis XVI and was executed during the French Revolution?
A) Marie Antoinette
B) Catherine the Great

17- Who was the Queen of England who was the daughter of King Henry VIII and Anne Boleyn?
A) Queen Elizabeth I
B) Queen Elizabeth II

18- Who was the Queen of Egypt who was the last ruler of the Ptolemaic dynasty and was known for her intelligence and political savvy?
A) Cleopatra
B) Nefertiti

19- Who was the Queen of England who ruled from 1553 to 1558 and was known for her persecution of Protestants?
A) Queen Elizabeth I
B) Queen Mary I

ANSWERS

1- Who was the Queen of England during World War II?
A) Queen Elizabeth II
B) Queen Elizabeth, the Queen Mother (Answer)

2- Who was the first female pharaoh of ancient Egypt?
A) Nefertiti
B) Hatshepsut (Answer)

3- Who was the Queen of France during the French Revolution?
A) Marie Antoinette (Answer)
B) Catherine the Great

4- Who was the Queen of Spain during the 16th century who supported Christopher Columbus' voyage to the Americas?
A) Isabella I (Answer)
B) Maria Theresa

5- Who was the Queen of Scotland who was executed by Queen Elizabeth I of England?
A) Mary, Queen of Scots (Answer)
B) Catherine of Aragon

6- Who was the Queen of England who ruled from 1558 to 1603 and oversaw a period of great cultural and economic growth?
A) Queen Victoria
B) Queen Elizabeth I (Answer)

7- Who was the Queen of Egypt who ruled during the Ptolemaic dynasty and was known for her beauty and intelligence?
A) Cleopatra (Answer)
B) Nefertiti

8- Who was the Queen of Sheba who visited King Solomon in the Bible?
A) Queen Esther
B) Queen of Sheba (Answer)

9- Who was the Queen of England who ruled from 1837 to 1901 and oversaw a period of great industrial expansion and colonialism?
A) Queen Elizabeth II
B) Queen Victoria (Answer)

10- Who was the Queen of England who was famously beheaded by her husband King Henry VIII?
A) Anne Boleyn (Answer)
B) Mary, Queen of Scots

11- Who was the Queen of Spain who supported the famous painter Diego Velázquez?
A) Isabella II
B) Isabella I (Answer)

12- Who was the Queen of England who ruled from 1603 to 1625 and sponsored the arts and literature during the Elizabethan era?
A) Queen Mary I
B) Queen Elizabeth I (Answer)

13- Who was the Queen of England who ruled from 1702 to 1714 and oversaw the War of the Spanish Succession?
A) Queen Anne (Answer)
B) Queen Victoria

14- Who was the Queen of England who was known as the "Virgin Queen" because she never married?
A) Queen Elizabeth I (Answer)
B) Queen Mary I

15- Who was the Queen of England who was known for her philanthropy and charity work, and ruled during the 19th century?
A) Queen Elizabeth II
B) Queen Victoria (Answer)

16- Who was the Queen of France who was married to King Louis XVI and was executed during the French Revolution?
A) Marie Antoinette (Answer)
B) Catherine the Great

17- Who was the Queen of England who was the daughter of King Henry VIII and Anne Boleyn?
A) Queen Elizabeth I
B) Queen Elizabeth II

18- Who was the Queen of Egypt who was the last ruler of the Ptolemaic dynasty and was known for her intelligence and political savvy?
A) Cleopatra (Answer)
B) Nefertiti

19- Who was the Queen of England who ruled from 1553 to 1558 and was known for her persecution of Protestants?
A) Queen Elizabeth I
B) Queen Mary I (Answer)

1- What is the name of the Spanish artist who co-founded the Cubist movement?
A) Salvador Dali
B) Pablo Picasso

2- What is the name of the painting by Picasso that depicts a tragic event during the Spanish Civil War?
A) Guernica
B) The Starry Night

3- What is the name of the artistic movement that Picasso helped create with Georges Braque?
A) Impressionism
B) Cubism

4- What is the name of the famous painting by Picasso that depicts five prostitutes in a brothel?
A) Les Demoiselles d'Avignon
B) The Scream

5- What is the name of the painting by Picasso that shows a distorted image of a guitar?
A) The Old Guitarist
B) Guitar

6- What is the name of the painting by Picasso that shows a woman sitting in a chair with a guitar in her lap?
A) The Guitar Player
B) The Night Watch

7- What is the name of the painting by Picasso that depicts a scene from a bullfight?
A) The Bullfighter
B) The Bullfight

8- What is the name of the painting by Picasso that shows a man with a guitar and a woman with a mandolin?
A) The Guitarist
B) The Scream

9- What is the name of the painting by Picasso that shows a woman sitting in a chair with a book in her lap?
A) Woman Reading
B) Mona Lisa

10- What is the name of the painting by Picasso that shows a woman with a flower in her hair?
A) Dora Maar au Chat
B) Head of a Woman

11- What is the name of the painting by Picasso that shows a woman sitting on a chair with her arms folded?
A) Seated Woman
B) The Thinker

12- What is the name of the painting by Picasso that shows a woman with a hat and a green face?
A) Woman with a Hat
B) The Weeping Woman

13- What is the name of the painting by Picasso that shows a woman with her hands covering her face?
A) Woman with Hands
B) Woman with Folded Arms

14- What is the name of the painting by Picasso that shows a group of people at a cafe?
A) Les Demoiselles d'Avignon
B) At the Lapin Agile

15- What is the name of the painting by Picasso that shows a man with a pipe and a woman with a flower in her hair?
A) Two Women with a Table
B) The Old Guitarist

16- What is the name of the painting by Picasso that shows a woman lying on a bed with a mirror behind her?
A) La Reve
B) The Persistence of Memory

17- What is the name of the painting by Picasso that shows a man playing a guitar?
A) The Musician
B) The Scream

18- What is the name of the painting by Picasso that shows a woman with a bird sitting on her shoulder?
A) Femme au Perroquet
B) The Kiss

19- What is the name of the painting by Picasso that shows a group of women on a beach?
A) Les Baigneuses
B) Water Lilies

ANSWERS

1- What is the name of the Spanish artist who co-founded the Cubist movement?
A) Salvador Dali
B) Pablo Picasso (Answer)

2- What is the name of the painting by Picasso that depicts a tragic event during the Spanish Civil War?
A) Guernica (Answer)
B) The Starry Night

3- What is the name of the artistic movement that Picasso helped create with Georges Braque?
A) Impressionism
B) Cubism (Answer)

4- What is the name of the famous painting by Picasso that depicts five prostitutes in a brothel?
A) Les Demoiselles d'Avignon (Answer)
B) The Scream

5- What is the name of the painting by Picasso that shows a distorted image of a guitar?
A) The Old Guitarist
B) Guitar (Answer)

6- What is the name of the painting by Picasso that shows a woman sitting in a chair with a guitar in her lap?
A) The Guitar Player (Answer)
B) The Night Watch

7- What is the name of the painting by Picasso that depicts a scene from a bullfight?
A) The Bullfighter
B) The Bullfight (Answer)

8- What is the name of the painting by Picasso that shows a man with a guitar and a woman with a mandolin?
A) The Guitarist (Answer)
B) The Scream

9- What is the name of the painting by Picasso that shows a woman sitting in a chair with a book in her lap?
A) Woman Reading (Answer)
B) Mona Lisa

10- What is the name of the painting by Picasso that shows a woman with a flower in her hair?
A) Dora Maar au Chat
B) Head of a Woman (Answer)

11- What is the name of the painting by Picasso that shows a woman sitting on a chair with her arms folded?
A) Seated Woman (Answer)
B) The Thinker

12- What is the name of the painting by Picasso that shows a woman with a hat and a green face?
A) Woman with a Hat
B) The Weeping Woman (Answer)

13- What is the name of the painting by Picasso that shows a woman with her hands covering her face?
A) Woman with Hands
B) Woman with Folded Arms (Answer)

14- What is the name of the painting by Picasso that shows a group of people at a cafe?
A) Les Demoiselles d'Avignon
B) At the Lapin Agile (Answer)

15- What is the name of the painting by Picasso that shows a man with a pipe and a woman with a flower in her hair?
A) Two Women with a Table
B) The Old Guitarist (Answer)

16- What is the name of the painting by Picasso that shows a woman lying on a bed with a mirror behind her?
A) La Reve (Answer)
B) The Persistence of Memory

17- What is the name of the painting by Picasso that shows a man playing a guitar?
A) The Musician (Answer)
B) The Scream

18- What is the name of the painting by Picasso that shows a woman with a bird sitting on her shoulder?
A) Femme au Perroquet (Answer)
B) The Kiss

19- What is the name of the painting by Picasso that shows a group of women on a beach?
A) Les Baigneuses (Answer)
B) Water Lilies

1- What is the scientific name for a hamster?
A) Cricetus
B) Hamsterus

2- What is the average lifespan of a hamster?
A) 2 years
B) 5 years

3- Are hamsters nocturnal or diurnal?
A) Nocturnal
B) Diurnal

4- What is the most common type of hamster?
A) Syrian hamster
B) Chinese hamster

5- What is the average size of a hamster?
A) 2-3 inches in length
B) 6-7 inches in length

6- What type of bedding is best for hamsters?
A) Cedar shavings
B) Aspen shavings

7- How many teeth do hamsters have?
A) 16
B) 24

8- Can hamsters see in color?
A) Yes
B) No

9- What is the gestation period for hamsters?
A) 3-4 weeks
B) 3-4 months

10- Do hamsters hibernate?
A) Yes
B) No

11- Can hamsters swim?
A) Yes
B) No

12- What type of food should be the mainstay of a hamster's diet?
A) Seeds
B) Fruit

13- Can hamsters be trained?
A) Yes
B) No

14- How many toes do hamsters have on their front paws?
A) 3
B) 4

15- Can hamsters live together in the same cage?
A) Yes
B) No

16- What is the name of the gland that produces a hamster's scent?
A) Sebaceous gland
B) Salivary gland

17- How often do hamsters need to be fed?
A) Once a day
B) Twice a day

18- What is the most common health problem in hamsters?
A) Obesity
B) Arthritis

19- What is the average weight of a hamster?
A) 50 grams
B) 100-150 grams

20- Can hamsters eat cheese?
A) Yes
B) No

21- What is the scientific name for a dwarf hamster?
A) Phodopus
B) Hamsterinus

22- What is the best temperature range for a hamster's environment?
A) 70-75°F
B) 65-68°F

23- Do hamsters need exercise wheels?
A) Yes
B) No

24- Can hamsters get fleas?
A) Yes
B) No

25- What is the name of the hamster in the movie "Bolt"?
A) Rhino
B) Mittens

ANSWERS

1- What is the scientific name for a hamster?
A) Cricetus (Answer)
B) Hamsterus

2- What is the average lifespan of a hamster?
A) 2 years
B) 5 years (Answer)

3- Are hamsters nocturnal or diurnal?
A) Nocturnal (Answer)
B) Diurnal

4- What is the most common type of hamster?
A) Syrian hamster (Answer)
B) Chinese hamster

5- What is the average size of a hamster?
A) 2-3 inches in length
B) 6-7 inches in length (Answer)

6- What type of bedding is best for hamsters?
A) Cedar shavings
B) Aspen shavings (Answer)

7- How many teeth do hamsters have?
A) 16
B) 24 (Answer)

8- Can hamsters see in color?
A) Yes
B) No (Answer)

9- What is the gestation period for hamsters?
A) 3-4 weeks (Answer)
B) 3-4 months

10- Do hamsters hibernate?
A) Yes
B) No (Answer)

11- Can hamsters swim?
A) Yes
B) No (Answer)

12- What type of food should be the mainstay of a hamster's diet?
A) Seeds (Answer)
B) Fruit

13- Can hamsters be trained?
A) Yes (Answer)
B) No

14- How many toes do hamsters have on their front paws?
A) 3
B) 4 (Answer)

15- Can hamsters live together in the same cage?
A) Yes (Answer)
B) No

16- What is the name of the gland that produces a hamster's scent?
A) Sebaceous gland (Answer)
B) Salivary gland

17- How often do hamsters need to be fed?
A) Once a day
B) Twice a day (Answer)

18- What is the most common health problem in hamsters?
A) Obesity (Answer)
B) Arthritis

19- What is the average weight of a hamster?
A) 50 grams
B) 100-150 grams (Answer)

20- Can hamsters eat cheese?
A) Yes
B) No (Answer)

21- What is the scientific name for a dwarf hamster?
A) Phodopus (Answer)
B) Hamsterinus

22- What is the best temperature range for a hamster's environment?
A) 70-75°F
B) 65-68°F (Answer)

23- Do hamsters need exercise wheels?
A) Yes (Answer)
B) No

24- Can hamsters get fleas?
A) Yes (Answer)
B) No

25- What is the name of the hamster in the movie "Bolt"?
A) Rhino
B) Mittens (Answer)